THE RESTLESS EARTH

EARTHQUAKES AND VOLCANOES

THE RESTLESS EARTH

Earthquakes and Volcanoes

Fossils

Layers of the Earth

Mountains and Valleys

Rivers, Lakes, and Oceans

Rocks and Minerals

THE RESTLESS EARTH

EARTHQUAKES AND VOLCANOES

Ellen Prager, Ph.D.

THE FRANKLIN INSTITUTE

CHELSEA HOUSE
PUBLISHERS
An imprint of Infobase Publishing

Library of Congress Cataloging-in-Publication Data
Prager, Ellen J.
Earthquakes and volcanoes / Ellen Prager.
    p. — cm.   (The restless Earth)
Includes bibliographical references and index.
ISBN 978-0-7910-9705-2 (hardcover)
1. Earthquakes. 2. Volcanoes. I. Title. II. Series.
QE521.P86 2008
551.21—dc22   2008008777

Text design by Erika K. Arroyo
Cover design by Ben Peterson

Printed in the United States of America

Bang FOF 10 9 8 7 6 5 4 3 2 1

This book is printed on acid-free paper.

Contents

▲ ▲ ▲

The Underlying and Shifting Earth

▲▲▲

FOR MOST PEOPLE, THE GROUND BENEATH THEIR FEET USUALLY STAYS quiet and still. It does not shake, rumble, or erupt skyward. Sometimes, however, especially in some regions, the Earth reveals its true nature as a restless and dynamic planet whose forces are both powerful and potentially destructive. Earthquakes can cause the ground to shake violently, roll, or rip apart. Even minor earthquakes can rattle homes and buildings. The danger increases in strong earthquakes, as does the potential damage. Bridges may collapse, roadways may be torn apart, and poorly built structures can give way. Earthquakes beneath the seafloor can also trigger dangerous and fast-moving tsunamis that pass through the open ocean without harm, but wreak disaster when they strike the shore.

There is just as much danger and violence when a volcano erupts. Earthquakes may rumble through the ground while huge amounts of ash blast skyward and turn day into night as the ash rains down on nearby towns. Blocks of fiery rock or lava may spew from a volcano's crater. Some volcanic eruptions become especially dangerous as they send searing clouds of deadly gas and debris into the air, or thick flows of mud down the volcano's slopes.

Yet, just as earthquakes and volcanoes cause destruction on our planet, they also help to create the land we live on, fertile soils for growing crops, an atmosphere rich in oxygen, and beautiful places to see and enjoy. While taking advantage of the planet's bounty and lands, we must also learn to live with its dangers. Millions of people reside in areas prone to earthquakes or live within the shadow of a sleeping volcano. And the number of people at risk grows as human populations increase and spread out across the land. We cannot stop earthquakes from happening or prevent volcanoes from erupting, but we can work to better understand how, why, and where these events occur. And with improved knowledge,

Buildings such as this row of townhouses were destroyed during the 1989 earthquake in San Francisco, California.

we can better determine the dangers and reduce the risks to those people who may be living in harm's way.

In the ancient past, when earthquakes shook the ground or volcanic eruptions blasted high into the sky, people looked to mythical gods or legends for explanations. They prayed and sacrificed what was precious to them to prevent future catastrophes. Today, we look to science for explanations, and years of research are paying off. We now have a much greater understanding of what causes earthquakes and volcanic eruptions, where they are most likely to occur, and how they happen. We have also learned important lessons from the disasters of the past. And with advances in technology, we can now better watch for the signs of a coming volcanic eruption and construct buildings that are safer in an earthquake.

The Earth supports life, yet it is a restless planet capable of creating powerful and destructive forces. By better understanding earthquakes and volcanoes, we can live in greater safety on this planet we call home.

MOVING PIECES

The Earth has been changing ever since its birth more than 4 billion years ago. Scientists believe that early in our planet's history, a process began that has created and shaped the surface features as we know them. Through time, this process has created our highest mountains and our deepest deep-sea trenches. It has shaped our coasts and islands and has controlled where the continents are located and where earthquakes and volcanoes are most likely to occur. It is a concept that has revolutionized earth science and provides the foundation upon which our understanding of the Earth and its powerful forces is now built. This concept is called *plate tectonics*.

The idea for plate tectonics first appeared as early as the fifteenth century, when the artist Leonardo da Vinci pondered how the edges of the continents seemed to fit together like the pieces of a jigsaw puzzle. As the centuries passed, mapmakers and geographers began drawing illustrations of how the continents could have looked if they were once pasted together into a giant supercontinent. Some thought that if the continents had once been fused together, maybe the supercontinent was broken up by a huge earthquake or gigantic flood.

In the early 1900s, Alfred Wegener, a young German **meteorologist**, came up with an idea that he called **continental drift**. Wegener proposed that the Earth's landmasses, or continents, could move both vertically and horizontally across the planet's surface. In his theory, he suggested that about 200 million years ago there was, in fact, a large supercontinent and that it had split apart about 100 to 150 million years ago. The continents then drifted apart while large ocean basins formed in between them. He based his theory on several interesting clues found in the **geology** of the continents.

Even though some continents now lie far apart from each other, Wegener noted that the fossils and rocks found on their

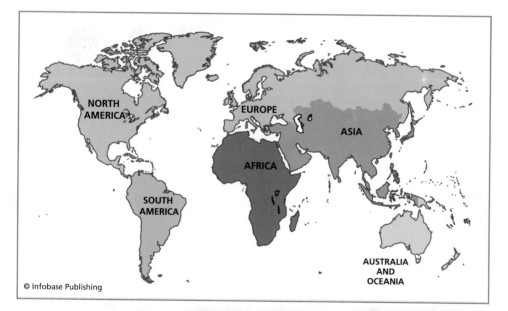

© Infobase Publishing

The shapes of continents look like a large jigsaw puzzle. In the world map above, notice how the continent of South America looks like it could fit next to the continent of Africa.

coasts are surprisingly similar. He suggested that these fossils and rocks are like the text on a newspaper that has been torn apart. If the pieces of the newspaper were pasted back together correctly, the edges would fit and the print would line up. For Wegener, the continents were like the newspaper, and the fossils and rocks were like the text, and so, at one time, they fit together. He also discovered rocks and fossils on some continents that were typically found in places with a much different **climate**. In the hot, dry valleys of Africa, he found geologic evidence of the influence of glaciers. In cold, polar regions, he discovered fossil ferns suggesting a climate that once had been tropical. For Wegener, these findings were evi-

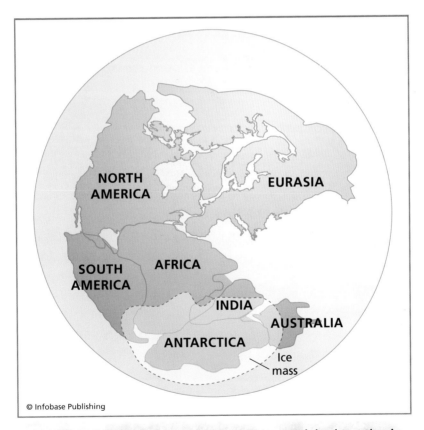

About 200 million years ago, the continents were joined together in one supercontinent. Over time, plate tectonics moved the continents into their present configuration.

dence not only that the continents had broken up over time, but also that they had drifted across the Earth's surface.

Unfortunately for Alfred Wegener, he proposed his theory of continental drift at a time when most scientists firmly believed that the land and oceans did not move and were eternally fixed in one place. Back then, geologists called Wegener's idea crazy and unbelievable. Wegener needed more substantial proof and a way to explain how the continents moved. Throughout his life, Wegener continued to search for evidence to support his theory. He died in 1930, during an expedition across the Greenland ice cap.

Many of Wegener's ideas have now been proven correct: The continents really have moved and shifted over the Earth's surface through time. There have been large supercontinents that broke up and big ocean basins that formed in between landmasses. Much of the proof for Wegener's ideas came with advances in technology that, for the first time, allowed for the detailed study of the ocean floor.

UNLOCKING THE SECRETS OF THE SEAFLOOR

After World War I, technology was developed to measure the ocean's depths by bouncing a pulse of sound off the seafloor and recording how long it took to echo back to the ship from which the pulse was sent. This technique was named echo sounding, or *sonar*. With the help of sonar, scientists began to make detailed surveys of ocean depth. By the 1950s, they came to a startling conclusion: There was an enormous undersea mountain chain encircling the globe. This chain is now known as the **mid-ocean ridge** system and is the world's longest mountain chain, wrapping around the globe for more than 37,280 miles (60,000 kilometers). On a map showing the topography of the seafloor, the mid-ocean ridge system appears like a huge undersea zipper across the planet's surface.

Following World War II, further advances in technology and an increased interest in the ocean and seafloor led to two more surprising discoveries. Using an instrument called a *magnetometer*, originally designed to detect submarines, scientists found strange

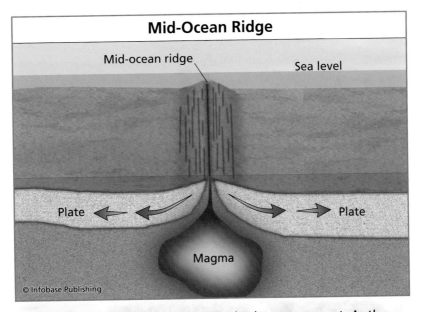

Mid-Ocean Ridge

Mid-ocean ridge

Sea level

Plate

Plate

Magma

© Infobase Publishing

A mid-ocean ridge is where two tectonic plates move apart. As the plates move apart, magma rises through the fractures at the axis of the ridge.

magnetic variations on the seafloor. When molten rock cools, the magnetic particles, or **minerals**, within it become aligned with the Earth's magnetic field. Throughout human history, the Earth's magnetic field has pointed to the north. (Magnets or magnetized materials are aligned, or point to, the north.) When oceanographers measured the magnetism in the rocks found around a mid-ocean ridge, however, they found a strange striped pattern running parallel to the ridge's centerline, or axis. Within these oddly striped patterns of magnetism was evidence that, in the past, the Earth's magnetic field did not point to the north as it does today, but pointed to the south; somehow, it was the reverse of what it is today. Scientists now believe that, in fact, the Earth's magnetic field has flip-flopped between north and south more than 100 times over the past 75 million years. The oceanographers who studied the seafloor were also surprised to find that there was a matching pattern, or mirror image, of magnetism on each side of the mid-ocean ridge's centerline.

Scientists at this time proposed a radical idea to explain the pattern in magnetism they had measured around the mid-ocean ridge: a process they called seafloor spreading. They suggested

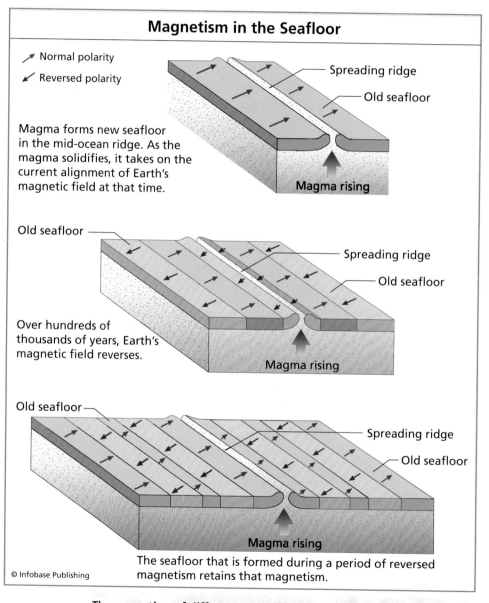

Magnetism in the Seafloor

Normal polarity

Reversed polarity

Spreading ridge

Old seafloor

Magma forms new seafloor in the mid-ocean ridge. As the magma solidifies, it takes on the current alignment of Earth's magnetic field at that time.

Magma rising

Old seafloor

Spreading ridge

Old seafloor

Over hundreds of thousands of years, Earth's magnetic field reverses.

Magma rising

Old seafloor

Spreading ridge

Old seafloor

Magma rising

The seafloor that is formed during a period of reversed magnetism retains that magnetism.

© Infobase Publishing

The magnetism of different parts of the seafloor indicates not only the rate of new seafloor being built by magma, but also records the reversal of the Earth's magnetic field over millions of years.

that new seafloor (or ocean **crust**) is created at the axis of a mid-ocean ridge by undersea volcanic eruptions. As the newly formed crust cools, it takes on the alignment of the current magnetic field. As the seafloor spreads, it slowly moves the new ocean crust away from both sides of the ridge axis. Over time, due to repeated reversals of the Earth's magnetic field and continued seafloor spreading, a similar zebralike pattern of magnetic stripes forms on each side of a mid-ocean ridge.

The idea of seafloor spreading was confirmed later when scientists used a specially designed drilling ship to collect samples of the ocean floor to determine its age. They found that the seafloor is youngest at the axis of a mid-ocean ridge and becomes increasingly older the farther away from the ridge they sampled. This confirmed the idea that ocean crust is formed at the ridge axis and then spreads outward over time. The oldest ocean crust they could find on the world's seafloor, however, was only 180 million years old. This raised a question: If the Earth is more than 4 billion years old, where did the older ocean crust go? Why didn't they find ocean crust as old as the Earth?

In 1965, Canadian scientist J. Tuzo Wilson came up with an idea that brought together Wegener's concept of continental drift and the idea of seafloor spreading, and also explained the mystery of the missing older ocean crust. He suggested that the stiff outer surface of the Earth is broken up into a number of moving pieces or plates. He further proposed that the formation of ocean crust at mid-ocean ridges is balanced by its destruction at **deep-sea trenches**. Deep-sea trenches are long, narrow, deep chasms in the seabed. The bottom of the Marianas Trench in the Pacific Ocean is more than 35,000 feet (10,900 meters) deep, the very deepest place in the sea. Wilson's theory explained why ocean crust older than 180 million years could not be found—because it was being destroyed or recycled back into the Earth at the deep-sea trenches. He also suggested that fractures found across the mid-ocean ridges, which he called **transform faults**, allowed for the motion of the relatively flat plates over the Earth's spherical surface. His idea that the Earth was divided into numerous plates was further supported by the distribution pattern of earthquakes and volcanoes, which indicated boundaries of extra geological activity.

Throughout the 1960s and 1970s, the evidence and support for Wegener's ideas and Wilson's theory grew and evolved into the concept that we now call plate tectonics. What was once considered a wild idea, then a theory, has become accepted science. Textbooks everywhere were rewritten and scientists throughout the world began to include plate tectonics in their lectures and research. The new realization that the planet's surface is more dynamic and complicated than once thought spurred questions and theories about the Earth's interior. And with this came one of the missing pieces in Wegener's original theory: the driving force for the movement of the continents.

INSIDE THE EARTH

Traveling into the Earth to see its interior remains a science fiction tale found in movies and books. Scientists are still unable to view the inside of the Earth firsthand, so they have had to devise other ways to unlock its geologic mysteries. For instance, they look for rocks from deep within the Earth that have been uplifted or ejected onto land or onto the seafloor. They drill deep into the ocean crust to collect samples for study. And, in the laboratory, scientists investigate how the extremely high pressures and temperatures that occur within the Earth affect the types of minerals and rocks we think might be there.

Much of what we know about the inside of the Earth comes from research on how seismic waves pass through the interior of the planet. **Seismic waves** are waves of energy that travel through the Earth and are typically generated by earthquakes or large explosions. The composition and physical structure of the Earth affects if and how fast these waves will pass through it. Scientists can learn more about the Earth's interior by studying these seismic waves.

In a simple but useful way, the Earth can be thought of as something like a spherical layer cake whose layers differ from each other in both chemical composition and physical structure. Think of vanilla versus chocolate cake and the differences between the textures of the somewhat fluid frosting as compared to the more solid cake (or chocolate versus vanilla). The chemical composition of the Earth can be roughly divided into three main layers. At the very center of the Earth is the **core**. Scientists think that the core is made of a very dense metallic material, probably a mixture of iron and nickel. Above the core is the **mantle**, a thick layer of dense rock that is rich in iron and magnesium. Above the mantle lies the Earth's crust. Compared to the other layers of the Earth (or, chocolate versus vanilla), the crust is extremely thin, like the

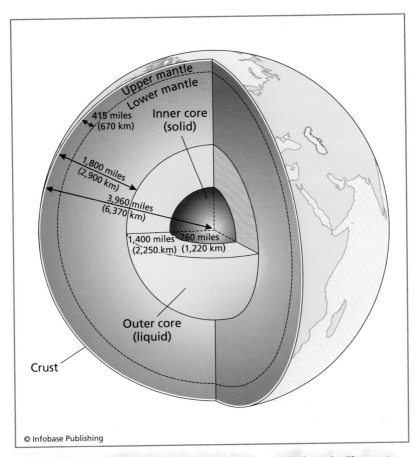

This cutaway model shows the internal structure of Earth. The center of the Earth has a solid inner core surrounded by a liquid outer core. The upper and lower mantle encircle the outer core. The crust is the outermost layer.

skin of an apple. The crust can be either **oceanic** or **continental** and includes all that we see on land or that lays beneath the sea. Continental crust is thicker, less dense, and composed of lighter minerals than oceanic crust. Oceanic crust, therefore, is relatively thinner, denser, and made of heavier minerals than continental crust. The boundary between the mantle and the crust is called the *Mohorovicic Discontinuity*, or simply, the "Moho."

The Earth's internal layering can also be viewed in terms of its physical structure (or, frosting versus cake), which is strongly influenced by changes in temperature and pressure. At the Earth's core, temperature and pressure are at their greatest. The core's temperature may be nearly as hot as the Sun's surface. While the Earth's entire core appears relatively similar in chemical composition, research suggests that it is split into an inner core that is solid and an outer core that is liquid. The spinning of the Earth about its axis and the motion this causes in the outer, metallic, liquid core is thought to create the planet's magnetic field.

Above the Earth's outer core is the rocky mantle. While much of the mantle appears to be hard, its exact physical nature remains uncertain. Some areas in the mantle appear to be somewhat molten, meaning that they are a thick **crystalline** mush that can flow very, very slowly. The upper half of the mantle contains a zone of molten material, called the **asthenosphere.** Relatively recent research suggests that a thin layer of molten material also exists at the boundary between the outer core and the mantle: Scientists call this the "D layer." Sitting above the asthenosphere is a rigid, somewhat brittle, and relatively thin layer called the **lithosphere**. It is made up of the top part of the mantle and the Earth's outer crust. The lithosphere is broken up into 15 large sections, or **tectonic plates**. These lithospheric or tectonic plates are irregular in shape, vary in size, and move in different directions over the Earth's spherical surface.

Two processes are now thought to drive the movement of the Earth's tectonic plates. One process begins with uneven heating and **convection** that takes place within the Earth's interior.

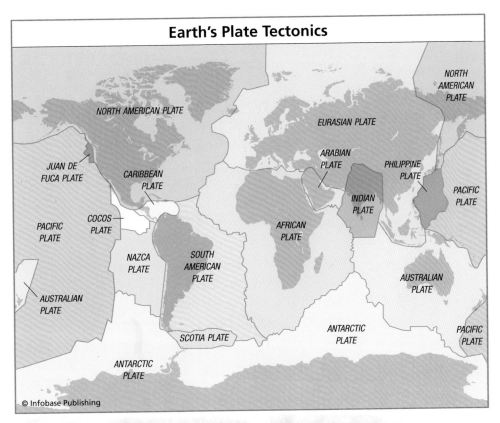

Earth's Plate Tectonics

NORTH AMERICAN PLATE

NORTH AMERICAN PLATE

EURASIAN PLATE

JUAN DE FUCA PLATE

CARIBBEAN PLATE

ARABIAN PLATE

PHILIPPINE PLATE

INDIAN PLATE

PACIFIC PLATE

PACIFIC PLATE

COCOS PLATE

AFRICAN PLATE

NAZCA PLATE

SOUTH AMERICAN PLATE

AUSTRALIAN PLATE

AUSTRALIAN PLATE

SCOTIA PLATE

ANTARCTIC PLATE

PACIFIC PLATE

ANTARCTIC PLATE

© Infobase Publishing

The Earth's surface is divided into large tectonic plates.

This causes plumes, or blobs of hot molten rock, to rise slowly through the asthenosphere toward the surface. At the base of the lithosphere, this rising molten rock is cooled, spreads out, and then sinks back into the mantle. The rising molten rock comes up under the mid-ocean ridges and the sinking material goes down beneath the deep-sea trenches. **Friction** between the asthenosphere and the overlying lithosphere acts like sticky tape, so that as the asthenosphere spreads out under the lithosphere, the tectonic plates are dragged along. Tectonic plates are also pulled along by slabs of oceanic crust as they are driven down (or "subducted") into the mantle beneath the trenches at what are called **subduction zones**.

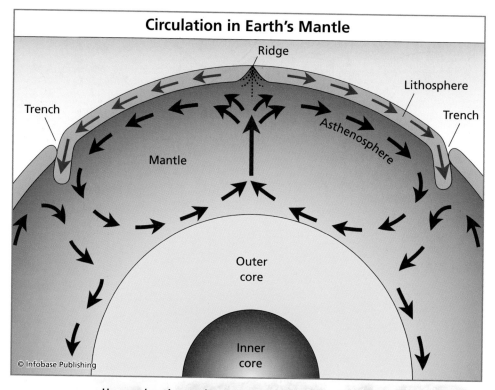

Circulation in Earth's Mantle

Ridge

Lithosphere

Trench

Trench

Asthenosphere

Mantle

Outer core

Inner core

© Infobase Publishing

Uneven heating and convection currents in the Earth's mantle force the molten rock of the mantle upward through cracks in the seafloor at mid-ocean ridges.

Undoubtedly, the inner workings of our planet are much more complicated than described here, but as more and more research is done, our understanding of the internal workings of the Earth will improve. One thing that we now know for sure: the Earth is a dynamic, moving planet, both in its interior and on the surface. And it is at the borders of the tectonic plates that most of the action takes place.

AT THE BORDERS

Each of the Earth's tectonic plates is part of the lithosphere, which is the very upper part of the mantle and the crust. A tectonic plate

(continued on page 24)

Convection

Convection is the transfer of heat through the movement of a fluid or gas. It occurs when an increase in temperature causes a liquid or gas to expand, to become less dense, and to rise within the surrounding material. An excellent example of convection occurs in a lava lamp. Heat from a light at the lamp's base warms colored wax in a surrounding oil mixture. As the wax heats up, it expands, becomes less dense, and rises in funky blobs, or a flowing plume, away from the source of heat at the base. By the time the wax reaches the top of the lava lamp, it has cooled enough to become denser than the surrounding oil and begins to sink back to the bottom of the lamp. At the base of the lamp, the wax absorbs heat, which is then released into the surrounding oil as the wax rises to the top of the lamp. The transfer of heat by the movement of the wax is an illustration of convection.

Convection is believed to occur within the Earth's interior. Heat from deep within the Earth causes plumes, or blobs of molten rock, to rise toward the surface in the asthenosphere. Scientists now believe that in some places, plumes may also rise from as deep as the boundary between the Earth's core and mantle.

A lava lamp displays an example of convection.

Hydrothermal Vents

In 1977, during a research cruise to study the Galapagos Rift Zone, an area of seafloor spreading off the coast of Ecuador, a team of scientists made an unexpected and startling discovery. They were investigating the possible presence of fractures in the seafloor, thousands of feet below the ocean surface, which emit warm water rich in chemicals and minerals and are known as **hydrothermal vents**. They found the vents all right, but then they made an even more surprising discovery.

The scientists first investigated the rift zone using an underwater robot. They towed this remotely operated vehicle (ROV) from their ship, just above the seafloor at depths of more than 8,000 feet (2,438 m). The ROV was equipped with special deep-sea cameras to take underwater photographs and instruments to measure temperature. Excitement among the scientists grew when an increase in water temperature was detected at the seafloor, because this suggested they had found a possible hydrothermal vent. When the photographs taken by the ROV's cameras came back, they also showed clusters of giant clams and hundreds of mussels on the seafloor. The scientists were shocked. Most people at the time thought that life in the deep sea was scarce.

The research ship *Lulu*, from the Woods Hole Oceanographic Institution, next arrived on the scene carrying a deep-diving **submersible** named *Alvin*. Two scientists and a pilot squeezed aboard *Alvin* to investigate the possible hydrothermal vent and the strange creatures that had appeared in the photographs. As the small submersible sank deep into the sea, the driver steered it toward the area of warm water. When they reached the seafloor, the scientists aboard *Alvin* could hardly believe their eyes. The area was crawling with life, and many of the creatures were completely new to science. Along with large clams, they saw white crabs, a purple octopus, and lush gardens of strange, long tubeworms with white stalks that were topped by bright red, feather-like gills. They had found an ecosystem in the deep sea that no one had ever seen or even imagined.

Scientists now estimate that there are about 280 active hydrothermal vent sites in the world's oceans. At the few hydrothermal vents that have been explored, researchers have discovered massive buildups of minerals that look like chimneys and can be as big as buildings. Some vents have super-hot, smoky-looking fluid, rich in chemicals and minerals, billowing out of them. Since they were first discovered, about 600 new species of marine life have been found thriving on the chemicals and bacteria associated with active hydrothermal vents.

Organisms such as the tubeworms and crabs pictured here thrive in biological communities surrounding hydrothermal vents.

(continued from page 20)

can contain oceanic crust, continental crust, or both. Because the plates move in different directions, independently of one another, they can collide, spread apart, and slip past each other. They can also bump, jostle, and even crumple up at their edges. It is this interaction at the edges of the Earth's tectonic plates that generates most of the world's earthquakes and where many of the deadliest volcanic eruptions happen. There are essentially three types of boundaries where plates meet: **divergent boundaries**, **convergent boundaries**, and **transform faults**.

Divergent Boundaries

The area where two tectonic plates are moving away from one another is called a divergent boundary. The mid-ocean ridges are a divergent plate boundary. As new ocean crust is created at the axis of a mid-ocean ridge, the tectonic plates on either side slowly spread apart. For example, in the Pacific Ocean, the East Pacific Rise is considered a fast-spreading mid-ocean ridge, moving apart at a rate of about 2 to 7 inches (6 to 17 centimeters) per year. In the Atlantic Ocean, the Mid-Atlantic Ridge is considered a slow-spreading mid-ocean ridge. It moves apart at a rate of about an inch or less (1 to 3 cm) each year. The structure of a mid-ocean ridge appears to be influenced by its spreading rate. Whereas the slow-spreading Mid-Atlantic Ridge has steep, blocky sides with a depression or valley at its center, the faster spreading East Pacific Rise is flatter and broader with a peak at its middle.

Convergent Boundaries

The area where two tectonic plates collide on the Earth's surface is known as a convergent boundary. When the edges of each colliding plate are made up of continental crust, these collisions result in the formation of towering mountains. These collisions are much like those where two automobiles crash head on, crumpling their front ends upward. About 50 million years ago, the collision of two plates, one with India at the front and the other containing Asia, created a huge mountain chain we now call the Himalayas. And because these plates are still converging, the Himalayas continue to rise, less than an inch (about 1 cm) each year.

When two tectonic plates collide and both of their front edges are made of oceanic crust, one of the plates will be forced—or subducted—under the other. The world's deep-sea trenches show surface evidence (or a clue) that a subduction zone lies below them. The Marianas Trench, the deepest trench on the planet, lies above where the Pacific Plate is being subducted under the Philippine Plate. When two plates containing oceanic crust collide, the older tectonic plate usually becomes subducted under the younger plate. This happens because as tectonic plates get older, they also become cooler and denser, so the less dense, younger plate tends to override the older, denser plate. Exceptions, however, do occur: For some unknown reason, in the Caribbean, the younger Caribbean Plate is being driven down beneath the older South American Plate.

In cases where one tectonic plate made of continental crust collides with a plate made of oceanic crust, usually the plate containing the denser oceanic crust is subducted beneath the plate containing the continental crust. For example, beneath the deep-sea Peru-Chile trench, the oceanic Nazca Plate is being driven under the continent of South America, which is part of the South American Plate. The collision of these plates has pushed up the land on the South American Plate to create the majestic mountain range called the Andes.

Sometimes when plates converge and one is subducted under the other, material from the downgoing slab may be scraped off and builds up onto the overriding plate. For example, the island of Barbados in the Caribbean is built on a wedge of **sediment** and rock scraped off the Caribbean Plate as it dives under the South American Plate.

Within the subduction zones of the world's convergent boundaries, many of the strongest earthquakes occur. Many of the planet's most powerful and explosive volcanoes also occur in these regions.

Transform Faults

The third type of plate boundary, where two plates slide past one another in opposite directions, is called a transform fault. The large fractures that slice across the mid-ocean ridges are considered transform faults. The most famous transform fault is called the San Andreas Fault and is found in California. Here, the northwest-moving Pacific Plate meets the southeast-moving North American Plate. As the two plates jostle, stick together, and slip along this transform fault, earthquakes periodically rock the surrounding land.

The science of the Earth has come a long way since people first started pondering the jigsaw puzzle-like fit of the continents. We now know that the Earth's surface changes over time, and that these changes are driven by plate tectonics. The movement of the Earth's tectonic plates will continue to shape and alter the surface of our planet and produce both earthquakes and volcanic eruptions.

The What and Where of Earthquakes

▲▲▲

EACH WEEK, ACROSS THE GLOBE, TWO TO THREE LARGE EARTHQUAKES take place. Lots of smaller earthquakes also occur. Most earthquakes are too small to feel, and many happen in areas where few people live. People typically think that in the United States, California has the most earthquakes. That dubious distinction, however, actually goes to Alaska. The Alaska Earthquake Information Center records about 22,000 earthquakes each year. While most of Alaska's quakes are small, big ones do happen. In 1964, for instance, one of the largest earthquakes ever recorded struck Alaska. This **magnitude** 9.2 quake struck in Prince William Sound and killed about 125 people. Anchorage and the surrounding towns suffered severe damage, with property losses estimated at more than $300 million. The great Alaskan quake also triggered a **tsunami** that killed people as far south as California.

California does have thousands of earthquakes each year as well, just not as many as Alaska. While most of these quakes are small, California has also had its share of major and destructive events. And with more people living in California than Alaska, these quakes are potentially far more deadly. Two of the worst

The 1964 Alaska earthquake ravaged this business-lined street in Anchorage.

California quakes were the 6.7 magnitude Northridge quake in 1994 and the infamous 1906 San Francisco quake that registered a magnitude of 7.8.

Strong earthquakes have also wreaked devastation outside of the United States. Their impact has been particularly severe in areas where buildings are not well constructed. In 2004, a massive 9.1 magnitude earthquake struck off the west coast of northern Sumatra, an island in Indonesia. The earthquake heavily damaged local villages and created a deadly tsunami that swept across the Indian Ocean. Hundreds of thousands of people were killed when the wave made landfall. Also catastrophic was a 2005 earthquake in Pakistan. That magnitude 7.6 quake killed at least 70,000 people and left about 3 million homeless. The largest earthquake ever recorded was a huge 9.5 magnitude quake that struck Chile in 1960.

Why is it that some places such as Alaska and California have more earthquakes than others? And what controls where the strongest earthquakes tend to occur?

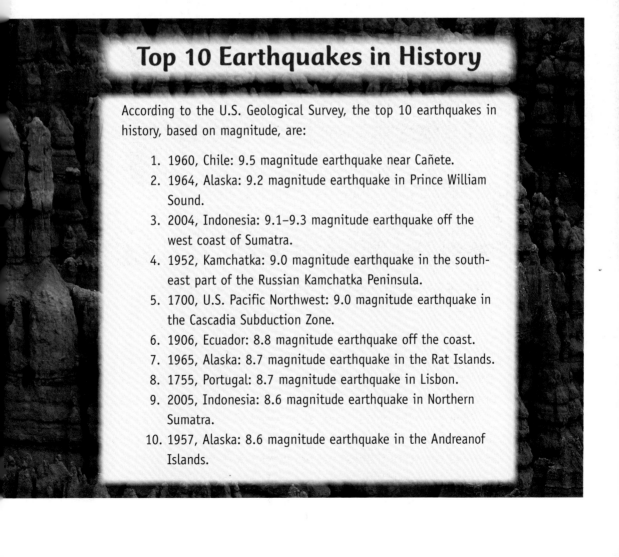

Top 10 Earthquakes in History

According to the U.S. Geological Survey, the top 10 earthquakes in history, based on magnitude, are:

1. 1960, Chile: 9.5 magnitude earthquake near Cañete.
2. 1964, Alaska: 9.2 magnitude earthquake in Prince William Sound.
3. 2004, Indonesia: 9.1–9.3 magnitude earthquake off the west coast of Sumatra.
4. 1952, Kamchatka: 9.0 magnitude earthquake in the southeast part of the Russian Kamchatka Peninsula.
5. 1700, U.S. Pacific Northwest: 9.0 magnitude earthquake in the Cascadia Subduction Zone.
6. 1906, Ecuador: 8.8 magnitude earthquake off the coast.
7. 1965, Alaska: 8.7 magnitude earthquake in the Rat Islands.
8. 1755, Portugal: 8.7 magnitude earthquake in Lisbon.
9. 2005, Indonesia: 8.6 magnitude earthquake in Northern Sumatra.
10. 1957, Alaska: 8.6 magnitude earthquake in the Andreanof Islands.

A GLOBAL PATTERN

If we plot the locations of the world's earthquakes over an extended period of time on a map, a striking pattern is revealed. Earthquakes are concentrated in certain areas and along lines that stretch across the globe. One arching band of earthquakes is particularly distinct, extending around the northern rim of the Pacific Ocean. This area of high earthquake and volcanic activity is called the Pacific "Ring of Fire." Lots of earthquakes also appear to occur in areas of the Middle East, in southern Europe, in Indonesia, and along what we now know are the world's mid-ocean ridges. With today's understanding of plate tectonics, the global distribution of earthquakes makes sense: They occur mainly along the edges of the Earth's tectonic plates.

The real key to understanding the relationship between earthquakes and the Earth's tectonic plates is the fact that most

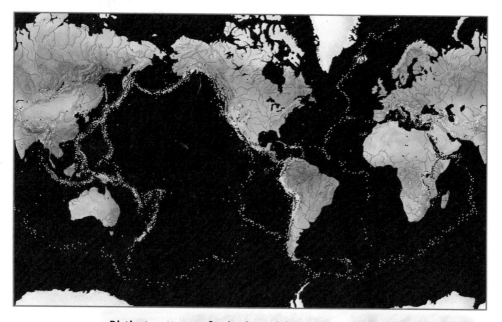

Distinct patterns of seismic activity emerge when viewing the location of Earth's volcanoes (*red triangles*) and earthquakes (*yellow dots*). Most dots and triangles are concentrated along the edges of the tectonic plates.

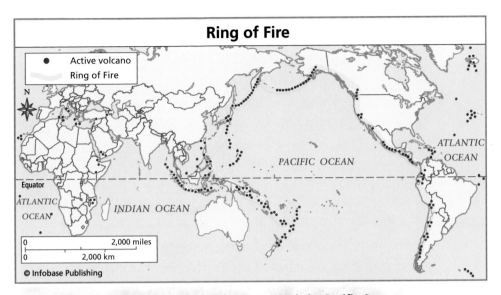

The Pacific Ring of Fire is made up of areas around the Pacific Ocean basin that are prone to volcanic and earthquake activity due to the Pacific Plate colliding with other tectonic plates.

earthquakes are caused by the movement of the tectonic plates. The earthquakes that occur at the mid-ocean ridges are caused by two tectonic plates that are moving apart. Those that occur at transform faults are caused by two plates that meet and move against one another in opposite directions. Where two tectonic plates collide is where we find many of the strongest and most frequent earthquakes, as with the Pacific's infamous Ring of Fire, where the Pacific Plate collides with its neighboring plates.

The Earth's tectonic plates move slowly across the planet's surface at about the same rate that your fingernails grow, give or take a little bit. At their boundaries, the plates bump and jostle against each other and sometimes get stuck together, or "locked," by friction. Because of this sticking, the surrounding crust becomes stressed, which causes the ground to bend or deform. At some point, the **strain** on the rocks becomes too great and they break. Breaking usually occurs along faults, which are thought to be areas in the crust that are relatively weak. The process is similar to stretching a rubber band. The farther it is stretched, the tighter it becomes. If stretched too far, the rubber band snaps. An earthquake occurs when the Earth's crust reaches its breaking point and snaps. The strain that has built up in the crust is released as energy that travels through the ground as vibrations, or seismic waves. The strength of the earthquake depends on how much energy is released.

Most earthquakes are relatively shallow and happen at a depth of less than 20 miles (32 km) within the Earth. Earthquakes can, however, also occur deeper, even as far down as hundreds of miles. Deep earthquakes occur most commonly in subduction zones, where one tectonic plate dives down beneath another. In fact, some of the world's strongest and most catastrophic earthquakes have occurred in subduction zones. The 1960 Chile, 1964 Alaska, and 2004 Sumatra earthquakes all occurred in subduction zones within or connected to the Pacific Ring of Fire.

In subduction zone earthquakes, the ground movement is typically vertical. For example, in 2005, an 8.7 magnitude earthquake struck two islands off of Sumatra. More than 900 people were killed and thousands were left homeless. During the earthquake, one part of an island was raised nearly four feet (1.2 m). A huge expanse of coral reef along the shore was lifted up and out of the ocean. Sumatra and its neighboring islands lie just north of a large subduction zone where the Australian Plate is being subducted under the Eurasian Plate. Because strong earthquakes associated with subduction zones can cause significant vertical movement of the seafloor, they may also trigger dangerous tsunamis.

The massive 2005 Pakistan earthquake occurred in another area of plate convergence, where the Indian Plate is colliding with the Eurasian Plate. This quake was particularly disastrous because many people lived in the area and most of the homes and buildings had been poorly built and were unable to withstand these events.

Earthquakes also occur along transform faults. The 1906 San Francisco earthquake struck along California's infamous transform fault, the San Andreas. The San Andreas Fault is more than 800 miles (1,820 km) long in its entirety and extends into the Earth at least 10 miles (16 km). In the past several decades, scientists have discovered that there are many smaller faults that branch off the San Andreas. In transform fault earthquakes such as those that take place on the San Andreas, the ground movement is mostly horizontal and can cause serious damage to roads, bridges, and buildings.

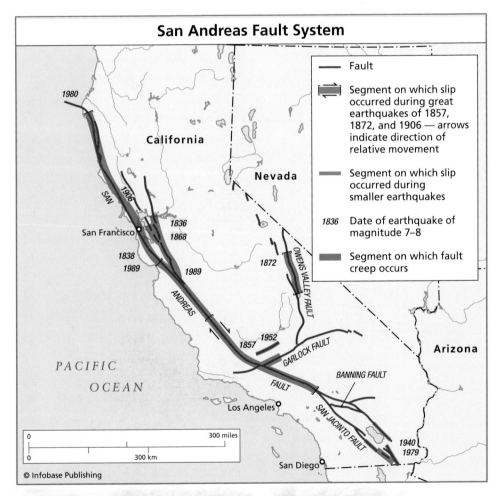

California's infamous San Andreas Fault

Though much less common, earthquakes can also occur on the interior of a tectonic plate. Scientists think that these types of earthquakes may be happening at old plate boundaries. For example, New Madrid, Missouri, which lies at the interior of

Magnitude

When it comes to an earthquake, how big is big? Today, we use the term *magnitude* to describe the size of an earthquake and to compare one quake to another. When the study of earthquakes was fairly new, the only way to quantify an earthquake's size was by how much damage it caused. We now call the amount of damage done by an earthquake its *intensity*. This is distinctly different from measuring its size or magnitude. For example, imagine that two earthquakes of the same size hit two different regions. In one area, many old brick homes collapse when the earthquake strikes. In the other area, there are few homes and all of them are built of sturdy materials that can stand up to the shaking. Although the earthquake was the same size in both regions, the intensity of the quake was much greater in the first area because the quake caused more damage there. The intensity of an earthquake, or its amount of damage, is influenced by factors other than an earthquake's size. These factors include the number of people living in the area, the geology of the land, and the types of buildings present. So, damage is not a good way to compare events, and that is why scientists came up with a better measure of size, known as magnitude.

Advances in technology helped to develop magnitude as a way to measure an earthquake's size based on the ground motion or shaking that it causes. An earthquake's magnitude does not vary from region to region or place to place. Magnitude is often based on the maximum amplitude, or size, of the peaks recorded on a seismometer during an earthquake. These peaks reflect the amount of ground motion caused by the earthquake.

the North American Plate, is thought to be the location of an old boundary. It is still famous for the unexpected earthquakes of 1811 and 1812, when a total of four powerful quakes struck. Because the underlying land was made up of soft sediment, the

In the 1930s, a seismologist named Charles Richter wanted to create a magnitude scale that was based on whole numbers and easy to use. To accomplish this, he proposed a "local magnitude" scale. This became known as the Richter Scale. It is the logarithm to the base 10 of the amplitude recorded on a specific type of seismometer located 62 miles (100 km) from an earthquake's epicenter. Today, we still use this same logarithmic scale, but it is based on the use of more advanced instruments, and there are now a variety of ways of measuring or calculating magnitude. Scientists now usually refer to an earthquake's size simply as magnitude and rarely use the term "on the Richter Scale." Using a logarithm scale to the base 10 means that for every whole number increase on the magnitude scale, the amplitude goes up by a factor of 10. In other words, the ground motion or shaking of a magnitude 5.0 earthquake will be 10 times the shaking of a magnitude 4.0 earthquake. However, the amount of energy released by a magnitude 5.0 earthquake as compared to magnitude 4.0 does not increase by 10, but rather by much more: in fact, 32 times more.

Following an earthquake, scientists examine the data from many seismic stations and use computers to compute the magnitude as accurately as possible. One type of magnitude, the moment magnitude, is based on a measure of how much and how far the Earth's crust actually shifts during a quake. Determining an earthquake's precise magnitude can take a bit of time. Typically, the magnitude of a quake will be revised several times after an event has occurred, as more data is obtained and analyzed.

Earthquakes are considered strong at a magnitude 6.0, major at 7.0. A great quake is when the magnitude is 8.0 or higher.

shaking was extremely strong. Witnesses described the ground as rippling like a field of wheat in the wind. Even the course of the Mississippi River was altered. In other areas, what was once dry land instantly turned into a lake or a swamp. Witnesses said that huge geysers of sand erupted skyward. The largest of the four New Madrid earthquakes was felt as far away as Boston and Washington, D.C. Luckily, at the time, there were relatively few people living in the area, and their sturdy log cabin homes stood up well against the shaking. As it turns out, New Madrid may lie over an old plate boundary or an associated fault.

Earthquakes also commonly occur along the mid-ocean ridges and areas of plate divergence. They are also associated with volcanoes.

FINDING THE EPICENTER

When an earthquake occurs, everyone wants to know where it happened and how big it was. Scientists can now rapidly answer these questions. They can determine an earthquake's magnitude based on the **amplitude,** or size, of the seismic waves detected and recorded on an instrument called a **seismometer**. They can also use the arrival time of the seismic waves to determine the quake's location, or **epicenter**. The exact location within the Earth where an earthquake occurs is called the **hypocenter,** or focus. The epicenter is the spot on the Earth's surface directly above the hypocenter. The epicenter is essentially the place where a rupture, or break, in a fault first starts during an earthquake. The tear in a fault can spread a long way from the initial starting point. In the 2004 Sumatra earthquake, scientists estimate that the fault rupture was more than 700 miles long (1200 km).

When a fault ruptures, the energy released travels through the Earth as seismic waves that radiate outward. It is somewhat like the waves that radiate outward from a stone thrown into a pond. There are several kinds of seismic waves. The fastest are P-waves, or primary waves. The first kind of seismic wave to be recorded on a seismometer during an earthquake, these are classified as compressional waves, meaning that they pass through materials by jiggling

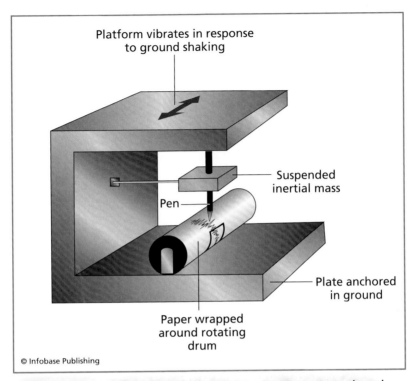

Platform vibrates in response to ground shaking

Suspended inertial mass

Pen

Plate anchored in ground

Paper wrapped around rotating drum

© Infobase Publishing

A seismograph is the older cousin of the seismometer, a tool used to measure the magnitude of earthquakes. In the seismograph diagram above, a weight suspended by a spring moves when vibrations are made. Attached to the weight is a pen that records the movement on a rotating drum.

molecules back and forth, in the same direction that they are traveling. If you take a long spring such as a Slinky, stretch it, and then tap one end of the spring, a wave travels down its length by moving sections to and fro. This action is similar to the compressional motion of a P-wave. P-waves can pass through both solids and liquids, and their speed increases as the density of the material they are passing through increases. Secondary waves, or S-waves, do not travel as quickly as P-waves. They are also called shear waves. They travel through the ground by deforming it or shifting the molecules from side to side. S-waves can pass through solids, but because true liquids cannot be deformed, they cannot pass through liquids.

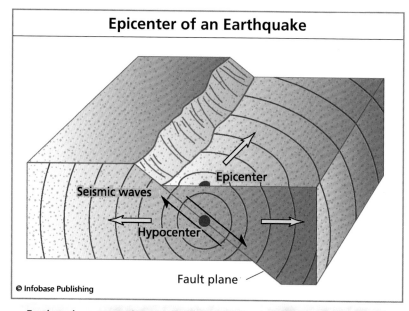

Epicenter of an Earthquake

Epicenter

Seismic waves

Hypocenter

Fault plane

© Infobase Publishing

Earthquakes occur along a fault. The area where an earthquake originates is called the hypocenter, or focus. Directly above the focus on Earth's surface is the epicenter. Seismic waves radiate from the focus.

Scientists across the globe have established specific stations to detect seismic waves. The seismometers used at seismic stations are now very sensitive and can detect different types of seismic waves, as well as earthquakes that are too small for a person to feel. They can also record the weak ground motion of a large, very distant earthquake or an explosion. An earthquake of magnitude 6.0 or higher can be detected by seismometers anywhere in the world. Some instruments are so sensitive they can pick up the nearby movement of trains, trucks, high surf, and even strong winds.

Scientists need to know the arrival times of P- and S-waves from at least three seismic stations to precisely locate an earthquake's epicenter. If they have data from a fourth seismic station, then the quake's depth within the Earth—its hypocenter, or focus—can also be determined.

Earthquake Science

▲ ▲ ▲

Scientists who study earthquakes are called **seismologists**. Seismologists investigate a wide variety of interesting topics related to earthquakes, such as how a fault ruptures during a quake or how the geology of the land affects the amount of shaking that occurs. Seismologists also study the pattern of aftershocks following an earthquake. They may assess what the probability of an earthquake is in a specific region or what the dangers are when one strikes. Seismologists also work closely with engineers and geologists to build roads, bridges, and buildings that will be safe during an earthquake. And, of course, there are scientists who are striving to find a way to predict earthquakes and to give people an early warning before they happen.

FAULTS

To better understand where and why earthquakes happen in a specific region, scientists often try to identify and map all of the faults present. As previously noted, faults are thought to be places in the Earth's crust that are relatively weak. These areas tend to break first when under enough strain. Faults can appear as large

The twisted curve of this train track in Guatemala indicates an offset in the landscape caused by the Motagua Fault.

cracks or fractures in the ground, offsets in the landscape, or they may lie underground, hidden from view. Some faults extend for hundreds of miles, while others cover a much shorter distance. Faults can also branch out into a series or system of faults.

Once a fault is discovered, seismologists want to know how much strain it is under. They may discover that the tectonic plates associated with the fault are creeping slowly but steadily. On the other hand, the tectonic plates may be stuck, locked in place by friction. If a fault is locked and strain is building up, then scientists want to know when that fault might rupture and cause an earthquake. They also want to know how much ground motion would be caused if an earthquake were to occur. If there is a history of earthquakes that have taken place on a specific fault in the region, information from past events can help to understand what future earthquakes may be like.

There are essentially three types of faults. A *strike-slip fault* is another means of describing a transform fault, where two tectonic plates are moving or slipping horizontally past each other in opposite directions. These faults are called strike-slip because the direction of the slip is parallel to the direction of the fault, or "strike," across the landscape. The second and third types, *normal* and *thrust* faults, both involve vertical motion. In places where the Earth's crust on either side of a fault is being pulled apart, such as at a mid-ocean ridge, one side of the fault may slide downward relative to the other. This is called a normal fault. A thrust fault is where the crust is being compressed with one side being forced up over the other. Thrust faults occur most commonly where tectonic plates are converging, such as in a subduction zone. Blind thrust faults are thrust faults hidden beneath the surface.

To study faults and how the Earth's crust moves before or during an earthquake, scientists today use a wide variety of high-tech tools, including global positioning system (GPS) receivers, seismometers, and satellite imagery. To determine how much of a fault ruptures or tears during an earthquake, scientists look at where aftershocks occur.

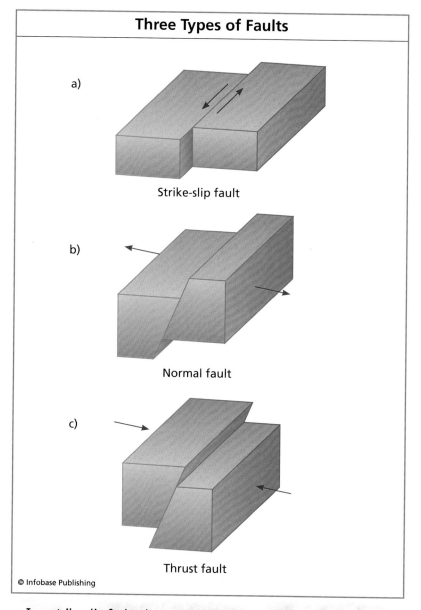

Three Types of Faults

a)

Strike-slip fault

b)

Normal fault

c)

Thrust fault

© Infobase Publishing

In a strike-slip fault, the movement of the plates is parallel to the fault (a). In a normal fault, one plate slides lower than the other plate (b). In a thrust fault, one plate is pushed up and over the other plate (c).

AFTERSHOCKS

Rarely does an earthquake happen singly, all by itself. While scientists define the largest earthquake in a series of quakes as the *mainshock,* smaller quakes that come before the mainshock are called *foreshocks* and those that happen afterwards are called *aftershocks.* Some earthquakes have foreshocks, while others do not. In the 1994 Northridge earthquake in California, the 6.7 magnitude mainshock was the largest quake, but there were no foreshocks. There were, however, thousands of aftershocks that began immediately after the mainshock and continued for about five years. Many of these aftershocks happened within the first month following the quake. Typically, aftershocks become less frequent with time. It is possible, however, to have a large and damaging aftershock several months after a major quake, but usually they come sooner rather than later.

People always want to know how long the aftershocks will last. Unfortunately, there is really no sure way of telling. Scientists often can make a pretty good guess about when the aftershocks might end, however, based on the history of earthquakes within a given region. The epicenters of the aftershocks that occur soon after an earthquake usually form a cluster or concentrate around an area of activity. Most of the time, this area outlines where a fault has ruptured during the main earthquake. A fault can rupture at one place and continue tearing in one direction, or it can break in two opposite directions. Some seismologists believe that an earthquake on one fault can also trigger breaks or earthquakes on other faults. The length and speed of a fault rupture influence the size of an earthquake and the damage it causes.

Aftershocks are essentially the ground adjusting to changes in the strain in the Earth's crust after an earthquake. Think about what happens when a piece of paper is crumpled into a ball and then set aside. The ball of paper crackles and uncrumples a bit, enlarging slightly in size, until it reaches a stable configuration. After an earthquake, the aftershocks are like the crackling and shifting of the paper ball. They continue until the Earth's crust becomes relatively stable. The release of strain on one portion of a fault can also cause strain or release on other parts of the

Cool Tools

From incredibly sensitive seismometers to earth-orbiting satellites and high-tech computer models, seismologists today have some very cool tools at their fingertips. Compared to the past, the instruments used today to detect and record earthquakes are much more precise and able to record much smaller earthquakes. Scientists can now use the GPS to accurately monitor and track the slow motion of the Earth's tectonic plates or detect ground deformation caused by strain. Scientists can also use radar images from satellites to compare pictures of the same location from two different dates and precisely calculate changes in the land surface. This can help scientists to locate faults or the movement of the Earth's crust associated with them.

Seismologists are also borrowing technology developed from the oil industry to help drill holes deep into the Earth to investigate faults, such as the San Andreas in California. Not only can they drill deep down, they can also drill horizontally at depth to take samples or install instruments. The advances in computer technology have also proven to be of great benefit for seismologists. With sophisticated computer models, they now can simulate earthquakes, fault movement, and ground shaking. By combining the information gained from a network of seismometers with computer modeling and graphics, seismologists now can create 3-D visualizations of the Earth's interior, of faults, and of earthquakes. This is called earthquake tomography and is something like the 3-D visualizations of the body done with CT scans, only in this case, scientists use seismic waves to create an image of the inside of the Earth. The science of earthquakes is advancing as the tools for research get better and better.

same fault or on nearby faults. Scientists often study sections adjacent to recently ruptured faults to look for areas that are at risk of breaking in the future and that could cause the next big earthquake.

SEISMIC CYCLE

As the Earth's tectonic plates shift and move over the planet's surface, there is an ongoing cycle of strain and release. Movement by the plates and friction at their edges causes strain to build up. When the strain becomes too much, the crust ruptures along weak points or faults. An earthquake occurs and the strain is released. The cycle then begins again as the tectonic plates continue to move and get stuck, and strain builds up again. Compared to the lifetime of a person, this seismic cycle happens over a much longer time period. In China and Japan, the written records of earthquakes go back thousands of years. In California, earthquake records go back only about 250 years. In terms of the history of the Earth and the movement of tectonic plates, these are very short time periods. We would understand more about the seismic cycle and earthquakes if we had records that extended further back in the Earth's history.

Scientists have discovered clever ways to learn about ancient earthquakes, those events where there are no written records or eyewitness accounts. Trees, sediment, and old stream or lakebeds that lie along a fault can sometimes provide clues about quakes that occurred a long time ago. Scientists studying the disruption of layered sediments within a lakebed along the San Andreas Fault near Palmdale, California, identified evidence of a dozen or so prehistoric earthquakes. Information on past quakes can help seismologists to understand how often big earthquakes tend to strike within a specific area.

Seismologists have long wondered if there are regular intervals or periods of time between earthquakes on specific faults. If the Earth's tectonic plates move at a relatively steady rate, and each fault is assumed to break at a certain level of strain, then one might be able to predict when a rupture or earthquake should occur. Unfortunately, it is not that simple. In the United States, however, there is one place in particular where scientists are focusing their efforts to better understand how often earthquakes happen and why.

PARKFIELD, CALIFORNIA

The town of Parkfield is located in central California on the San Andreas Fault. Scientists have been studying earthquakes in Parkfield since the 1970s. In 1984, their research had suggested that moderate-sized earthquakes occurred in the region about every 18 to 26 years. Based on this information, seismologists predicted that another earthquake would strike the Parkfield area around 1988, give or take about 4 years. Over the next several years, the area was equipped with all sorts of instruments to monitor and record the earthquake that many thought was coming. The major earthquake that was predicted has yet to happen.

Still, Parkfield continues to be the focus of intense research on earthquakes. There is currently an ongoing and ambitious effort to create a San Andreas Fault Observatory in the area. As part of the project, in 2004, the National Science Foundation and the U.S. Geological Survey (USGS) began drilling a hole into the fault to install instruments 1 to 2 miles (2 to 3 km) below the Earth's surface in a location near where magnitude 6.0 earthquakes have previously occurred. Studies done at the San Andreas Fault Observatory are revealing new information about the geologic structure of the San Andreas Fault. Seismologists are learning about how sections of the fault creep and about the role of very small earthquakes, which are called microearthquakes. They are also determining how much strain is building up on different parts of the San Andreas Fault in Parkfield and producing new computer-derived images of the fault. If a moderate to large earthquake does occur in the region, as is expected, it will probably be the best monitored and studied earthquake ever.

PREDICTING EARTHQUAKES

California has dozens of faults, some of them big, some of them small. Each earthquake that occurs in California relieves strain on some faults while possibly increasing strain on others. The result is that, even in an area so well studied, predicting where and when earthquakes are going to happen is a complicated and uncertain task. Seismologists cannot yet predict exactly where and when the next earthquake in California will take place or how big it will be. Based on the history of earthquakes in the region, however, and with our improved understanding of the processes involved, seismologists can forecast the possibility of an earthquake happening over a given length of time. For example, the chances of a magnitude 7.5 or larger earthquake (called the "Big One") occurring on the San Andreas Fault during the next 30 years is at least 50–50. In other words, there is just as good a chance that it will happen as that it will not. For an individual living in, or moving to, an area near the San Andreas Fault, this does not seem very helpful. For an engineer who plans to design a bridge, a road, a home, a large building, or anything that is expected to last at least 30 years, however, this is important information. An engineer must take into account the possibility of the strong shaking that can accompany an earthquake.

Will seismologists ever be able to predict earthquakes with more accuracy and provide people with more timely warnings? Unfortunately, the answer seems to be no, at least not anytime soon.

One of the problems with predicting earthquakes is that there is still a lot we do not fully understand or know about what goes on in the Earth's interior. It certainly does not help that we cannot see directly down inside the Earth and witness what is happening day to day or view what happens when an earthquake strikes. Most of our measurements are made at or near the surface, and we have to guess what is going on below from the study of these surface measurements. Some seismologists think that earthquakes will never be predictable. In short, they are naturally unpredictable.

Throughout history, as people have searched for a way to predict or forecast earthquakes, they have looked for early warning signs. Foreshocks could be an early warning sign of a larger earthquake to come, but some earthquakes do not have foreshocks. And some small earthquakes are just small earthquakes, not foreshocks that lead to a larger earthquake. There have also been reported changes in the level, flow, or temperature of **groundwater** before an earthquake. These types of changes do not always take place before an earthquake, however, and there are many other influences on groundwater change, such as rainfall, drought, and pumping. Changes related to electrical or magnetic fields have also been described before earthquakes. In regions where power lines and radio interference are everywhere, however, it can be difficult to accurately detect or measure minor electrical and magnetic changes. There are also many stories about animals behaving strangely just before a quake. There are a lot of outside influences on animal behavior as well: How can we know what causes a dog, or other animal, to act oddly?

In 1975, scientists measured hundreds of small earthquakes in Haicheng, China. They also detected changes in groundwater and people reported strange animal behavior. A major earthquake was forecast and orders were given to evacuate. Not long after, a magnitude 7.3 earthquake struck. The quake had accurately been predicted, and many lives were saved. Unfortunately, just one year later, no such timely prediction was made for a 7.8 magnitude earthquake that struck Tangshan, China. About 250,000 people reportedly perished in that disaster.

The bottom line is that scientists cannot yet say exactly where and when earthquakes will strike. New theories and ideas continually arise about how to forecast quakes or what the early warning signs are, but to date, none have proven reliable. Researchers are trying to more accurately pinpoint locations around the world where the potential for a major quake is high—for instance, in areas where strain has been building up on a major fault for a long period of time. Even so, no one can say exactly when and where the next big one will strike.

SEISMIC HAZARDS

Although we cannot yet reliably predict earthquakes, there are ways that we can help to save both lives and property. Within a given region, this often begins with identifying where the dangers are. Scientists often start by mapping the faults within a region and then assessing the size of the earthquakes that could occur. A wide variety of techniques can now be used to locate faults. In the 1990s, when scientists were mapping the faults near Portland, Oregon, they used a specially designed airplane equipped with instruments to measure the Earth's magnetic field. In their search for distinct patterns in the magnetic field that can indicate the presence of faults or breaks in the Earth's crust, they discovered a previously unknown fault that runs directly under the city of Portland.

Once the faults within a region have been identified, they are plotted on a seismic hazard map, which helps to identify where earthquakes are most likely to occur. Scientists are also producing maps of the ground shaking that occurs or is expected to occur during an earthquake. Ground shaking is influenced by a number of factors, including the size of the earthquake, the distance from the epicenter, and the underlying rock and soil types. After an earthquake, the USGS can now quickly produce maps that show the pattern of ground shaking. These maps can help emergency responders decide where to go and where the greatest damage may be. They can also provide the public with helpful information for planning and preparation efforts and aid in the design of highways, bridges, and buildings. They can also assist in estimating the possibility of landslides in earthquakes. Ground motion information is particularly important for areas like the city of Seattle, Washington, that sit on a basin of **sedimentary** rock.

Soft sediments, especially loose landfill, can greatly increase how much the ground shakes during an earthquake. And strong shaking can turn water-rich sand into quicksand. In the 1989 Loma Prieta earthquake in California, San Francisco's Marina District was devastated even though it was 62 miles (100 km) away from the epicenter. The Marina District was an upscale, trendy neighborhood, but it had been built on unstable sediments and landfill. Much of the underlying fill was actually rubble from the famous 1906 San Francisco quake. During the Loma Prieta quake, shaking caused the soft landfill within the Marina District to act like quicksand. Buildings and homes were destroyed or badly damaged as they sank or collapsed into the ground.

Earthquakes can also trigger landslides, flooding, fires, tsunamis, and possibly volcanic activity. It is difficult to predict if and when these types of problems will occur, but they must be considered in planning and preparing for earthquakes. Vital services such as water and gas lines, freeways, power lines, and railroads must also be considered. The damage to any of these "lifelines" in an earthquake can have severe consequences for people living in the region.

REDUCING RISK

Across the globe, scientists are working to help reduce the risks that earthquakes pose to people. They cannot stop earthquakes from happening, but they can help people build safer homes and become better prepared. There are now specialists in California who help homeowners quake-proof their property and reduce the dangers inside, such as heavy objects that could fall during an earthquake. On a larger scale, engineers work to improve the safety of home construction, especially in areas at high risk of earthquakes. In the United States, many homes have wood frames, which are lightweight and strong. When attached to their foundations, these wood-frame houses survive well in an earthquake. Older homes that are not bolted to their foundations do not fare as well. Buildings that have little reinforcement and are made of brick or other masonry often sustain the worst damage in earthquakes. In many other parts of the world, homes are traditionally built of stone or adobe, which crumble easily during quakes. In these areas, quakes of any magnitude can become tragic disasters due to the collapse or destruction of buildings, homes, and even schools, such as the tragic school collapses in the Sichuan province of China during the 7.9 magnitude earthquake that struck in May 2008.

Earthquakes have long been of great concern in Japan. Like other places in the world, Japanese scientists have yet to come up with a way to reliably predict earthquakes. They have, however, developed an experimental early warning system to provide an alert seconds before a quake strikes. The system is designed to detect the arrival of the fastest seismic waves, the P-waves. P-waves

Earthquake Safety

Earthquake safety begins with education and preparation. It is especially important to be prepared if you live in places such as Alaska or California, where earthquakes are more common. Earthquakes can happen in many areas, however, and even if you do not live in a region that is at high risk, you may one day be visiting an area when an earthquake strikes. Here are just a few tips to help. The Web sites listed at the back of the book provide more information.

During an earthquake:

- If you are indoors, drop down to the floor and take cover under something sturdy, like a desk or table. Be sure to stay away from windows, fireplaces, or objects that could fall from shelves or cabinets.
- If you are outdoors, go to an open space away from buildings and power lines. If you are driving in a car, stay inside, but stop and be sure you are away from bridges, overpasses, and tunnels. Try to stay away from traffic as well as trees, light posts, and signs that could fall. If you are near a cliff or rocky area, stay clear of where rocks could fall or slopes could give way. If you are on a beach, move quickly, but calmly, inland and to higher ground.
- Stay calm and listen to instructions from your parents, teachers, or emergency responders. If you or your family need help, call your local police or fire department, or dial 911.

arrive before the slower S-waves, which cause the most destructive ground shaking in large earthquakes. Systems that detect arriving P-waves are designed to send out an alert before the S-waves arrive. Even so, the warning will only come seconds before the S-waves arrive and the ground starts to really shake. It is hoped that these alarms will give enough warning time to automatically shut off gas and water lines or to stop trains. These warning systems could also give enough time to set off sirens or to send an alert through cell phones. Scientists and emergency responders in California are also working on ways to better warn the public and protect vital lifelines and services. Some people debate the usefulness of an early warning system with such short notice. Some also worry that it could also set off an unnecessary panic.

Our understanding of the Earth and earthquakes is better than ever before. We now know where earthquakes are most likely to occur and how severe the ground shaking is likely to be. We understand more today than in the past about the behavior of soils and manmade structures in earthquakes. We now have an increasingly improved earthquake monitoring system, and scientists are working to provide as timely warnings as possible. There are also efforts to educate people about the dangers of earthquakes and about how to build safer buildings. More still needs to be done, however. When a long time has passed without a large earthquake striking, people forget the dangers. Even people living in California can become neglectful. And for the millions of people who live in the world's poorer and more remote regions at risk, most go unprepared. They are especially vulnerable. We need to continue our efforts throughout the world to learn more about earthquakes and better prepare for them, so that people are as safe as possible when the Earth's restless nature causes the ground to rock and roll.

Undersea
Earthquakes
and Tsunamis

▲ ▲ ▲

IN LATE DECEMBER 2004, A MASSIVE EARTHQUAKE OFF THE ISLAND of Sumatra triggered a tsunami that killed hundreds of thousands of people. In the aftermath of this horrible disaster, people across the globe became much more aware of tsunamis and the dangers they pose. Tsunamis have been happening on planet Earth throughout its restless history. They are less common than earthquakes or volcanic eruptions, but they are potentially just as powerful and just as destructive.

Tsunamis are seismic sea waves. Sometimes they are called tidal waves, but they have little to do with the tides, so it is more accurate to call them tsunamis, which comes from the Japanese words *tsu*, meaning "harbor," and *nami*, meaning "wave." Tsunamis can be one or a series of waves generated by the sudden movement, or disturbance, of the seafloor. Earthquakes, volcanic eruptions, landslides, or asteroid impacts can trigger a tsunami. During the last decade or so, researchers have discovered that many tsunamis are generated when earthquakes cause underwater landslides. The largest tsunami ever recorded occurred in Lituya Bay, Alaska, in 1958 when an 8.0 magnitude earthquake

Survivors walk through the devastated city of Banda Aceh in Indonesia five days after the 2004 Indian Ocean tsunami.

struck 13 miles (21 km) away and triggered a huge landslide into the bay. This landslide created waves estimated to have reached an incredible 1,500 feet (450 m) in height.

Strong, shallow earthquakes under the seafloor are the most likely triggers of a tsunami. In fact, if an earthquake registering 7.0 magnitude or greater happens near the coast anywhere in the world, scientists automatically go on the alert for a tsunami, especially if it takes place near subduction zones where the faults involved tend to create vertical movement of the seafloor during

2004 Indian Ocean Tsunami

On December 26, 2004, a great quake struck about 155 miles (250 km) south of the island of Sumatra in Indonesia. The magnitude of the earthquake is now believed to have been between 9.1 and 9.3. The earthquake occurred in the subduction zone underlying the Sunda Trench at a depth of about 19 miles (30 km) and triggered one of the most powerful tsunamis ever recorded. It swept over nearby islands and across the Indian Ocean. About 300,000 deaths have been attributed to this tsunami, making it one of the worst catastrophes of our time.

This was not the first time an earthquake had generated a deadly tsunami in the region: Several tsunamis occurred in the 1800s. The magnitude of this event and its destruction, however, were unlike anything seen in recent history. The fault rupture associated with the earthquake that triggered the tsunami was more than 700 miles (1200 km) long. The rupture progressed in a north-to-northwest direction along the fault and may have focused the most powerful waves in a similar direction. The amount of energy released during the earthquake has been estimated to be the equivalent of 32 billion tons of TNT.

The tsunami struck within minutes along the northwest shores of Sumatra, but it took hours for the powerful waves to strike regions farther away. Because tsunamis are sudden, unpredictable, and infrequent, satellites are usually of little use in tracking them. Purely by coincidence, however, approximately two hours after the massive Sumatran earthquake, a U.S.-French satellite equipped with an instrument that estimates the height of the sea surface happened to pass over the region. The estimates from this instrument confirmed that the tsunami traveled as low waves, only about 1 to 2 feet (40 to 50 cm) high, through the open ocean. Scientists were able to differentiate the tsunami waves from the regular sea level by

(continued)

(continued)

comparing images from December 26, 2004, to images taken days or weeks before.

An international team of scientists was deployed after the tsunami struck. In Sri Lanka, they found that water from the tsunami flooded more than one-half mile (1 km) inland. Based on eyewitness accounts and evidence at the scene, the tsunami was 9 to 30 feet (3 to 10 m) high when it reached the shore in Sri Lanka.

Today, scientists and their partners within the international community are trying to better prepare the people who live along the shores of the Indian Ocean for tsunamis. One way is through the establishment of an effective warning system. Scientists also are trying to educate people about how to build safer structures, what the warning signs of a tsunami are, and how to prepare and respond. More investment in education, preparation, and emergency communications is needed if we are to prevent catastrophes of this size from happening again when the next monster tsunami comes to call.

an earthquake. Not all large quakes that take place under the seabed, in a subduction zone, or along the coast produce tsunamis. In general, the amount of vertical movement caused by an earthquake is thought to determine why some quakes trigger tsunamis while others do not.

In addition to an earthquake's size, the depth at which it occurs is also important in determining if it will trigger a tsunami. The deeper the earthquake, the less energy that reaches the surface, so there tends to be less vertical movement of the seafloor. Earthquakes that occur deeper than about 19 miles (30 km) rarely trigger a tsunami. Truly great quakes, however, such as the 9.5 magnitude quake that struck in Chile in 1960, can occasionally produce tsunamis even at great depths. An earthquake whose epicenter is on land can trigger a tsunami only if it produces vertical movement of the seafloor, or if it causes a large landslide into the sea, as happened with the quake in Lituya Bay, Alaska.

Vertical movement of the seafloor causes a tsunami by displacing the water above it. Imagine a small, inflated kiddie pool made of soft, flexible rubber. If you were to slide your hands under the bottom of the pool and lift up, the water would bulge up and then slosh to the sides of the pool. This is sort of what happens when an earthquake triggers a tsunami. If the seafloor is lifted up during the quake, it creates a hill of water overhead. Gravity causes the hill of water to collapse and sends waves traveling toward shore.

In the open ocean, tsunamis travel as fast, low, long waves, and although they appear similar to other waves in the sea, they are very different and much more deadly. Most waves in the ocean are created by the wind. In both wind waves and tsunamis, the horizontal distance between the crests, or peaks, of the waves is called the wavelength. The wave period is the time it takes for successive peaks to pass a fixed point. The wave height is the vertical distance from the wave trough to its crest. The wavelength of a tsunami can be hundreds of miles long, and the time between the crests of a tsunami—its period—can be anywhere from 10 minutes to more than an hour. Wind waves have much smaller wavelengths and their periods are typically less than 30 seconds. In the open ocean, wind waves can vary in height from just tiny ripples at the surface to rare rogue waves more than 90 feet (30 m) tall. In contrast, tsunamis race across the open ocean as a series of long, low-crested waves, usually less than 1 to 6 feet (1 to 2 m) high. (People on a ship out at sea would be completely unaware if a deadly tsunami were to pass beneath them. To them, the tsunami would seem like any other ocean wave.)

Wind waves transfer energy through the ocean mainly at the surface. Tsunamis, on the other hand, carry energy throughout the water from the seafloor to the surface. Wind waves tend to get smaller and lose energy as they move away from the area where they were formed. Tsunamis, on the other hand, do not lose energy while traveling through the ocean until they reach shore.

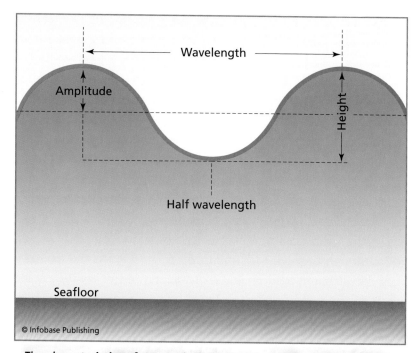

The characteristics of a wave include: wavelength, or the horizontal distance from the top of one wave crest (or peak) to another; height, or the vertical distance from the trough, or valley, to the top of the crest; and amplitude, or the vertical distance from the wave's midline to the top of a crest.

AT THE SHORE

Tsunamis are most often generated in relatively deep water. They then travel through the open ocean into shallow water and strike the shore. If tsunamis are triggered relatively close to shore, they can strike within minutes, with little warning. Tsunamis that are generated far from the coast can take hours to reach the shoreline. In the open ocean, the long, low waves of a tsunami travel as fast as a jet airplane, at speeds more than 400 miles per hour (700 kilometers per hour). Their speed is strongly dependent on the depth of the water. When a tsunami enters shallow water, it begins to "feel the bottom," or slow down. In depths of about 100 feet (30 m), a tsunami slows down to about 37 miles per hour (60 km/hr). It is important to note that even though a tsunami slows down at the shore, it still moves faster than a person can run.

As a tsunami slows down at the coast, it also gets shorter and steeper. The portion of the wave nearest the beach slows down as the seafloor becomes more shallow, but the back of the wave keeps going at a faster speed. This causes the wave to bunch up and become higher and steeper. At some point, the wave gets too steep, the top rides over the bottom, and it breaks. Essentially, the wave trips over its own feet. And because a tsunami's wavelength—the distance between peaks—is so long, a whole lot of water bunches up.

When they reach shore, tsunamis can form towering peaks or powerful surges of water. In either form, they release huge amounts of energy. Typical wind waves can erode beaches or create strong currents, but the energy of tsunamis can snap trees like twigs, destroy entire villages, and carry boats far inland. For example, 30 minutes after the huge 1883 eruption of the volcano on the island of Krakatau in Indonesia, people on the west coast of the island of Java reported seeing huge mountains of water rolling toward shore. The volcano's eruption had triggered a monstrous tsunami, possibly 98 feet (30 m) high when it rolled ashore. Trees and houses were totally destroyed. The tsunami carried a gunboat two miles inland and deposited it in the trees. About 32,000 people were reportedly killed.

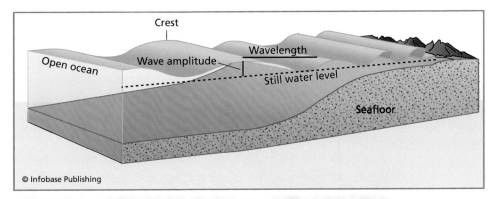

© Infobase Publishing

As a tsunami reaches shore, its wavelength shortens and its height grows taller, resulting in enormous waves or powerful surges when it makes landfall.

In addition to the danger that occurs when a tsunami strikes the shore, there is also great danger when the water that has been pushed inland flows swiftly back into the ocean, taking everything in its path with it.

As tsunamis move toward the coast, they continually change their form as they pass through varying depths of water and over the complex landscape of the seafloor. A tsunami that is generated by an earthquake off Hawaii may look one way when it strikes the coast of Hawaii and then take a very different form when it comes ashore on the beaches of California. For scientists who study tsunamis and people who issue warnings, these changes can be extremely hard to predict.

TSUNAMI SCIENCE

Tsunamis are difficult to study because they happen infrequently, occur suddenly, and are unpredictable. When a tsunami does strike, scientists try to learn as much about it as possible. In the aftermath of a tsunami, an international team of tsunami experts is often sent. These scientists interview eyewitnesses and look for clues about the height of the wave when it reached land and how far inland it flowed. The tsunami may have left behind a flood line on buildings that marks how high the water rose. Scattered piles of debris may also show how high the water rose or how far inland it flooded. In some cases, the destruction of homes and vegetation provides important clues as to how big and strong the tsunami was when it struck the shore. Scientists also examine the shape of the coastline, the water depth, and the habitats along the shore. All of these factors can affect how a tsunami impacts the coast. In recent years, scientists have discovered that the presence of healthy mangrove forests and coral reefs along the coast can help to buffer the impacts of a tsunami.

Scientists also take ships out to sea to investigate the movement of the seafloor they suspect triggered the tsunami, or to find out if a landslide was involved. The information they collect can help to better understand and model tsunamis and to help prepare and protect people for future events.

Computer modeling is now an important tool for tsunami scientists. Modeling helps scientists understand how tsunamis behave in different settings and assists in providing more accurate and timely warnings. A computer simulation of a tsunami is a combination of an earthquake, wave, and flood model. It requires the input of lots of information, including the size, depth, and location of a triggering earthquake, as well as the movement of the seafloor it produces. Scientists also need information about the depths of the ocean and any seafloor features over which the tsunami may pass. To accurately simulate how a tsunami strikes the coast, scientists need to know the shape of the shoreline, the orientation of the waves when they hit, and any habitats or structures that may be present. Overall, it is a complicated and difficult task. Computer simulations of tsunamis are improving rapidly and becoming an important way of studying, preparing for, and warning of potential disasters.

Scientists also study tsunamis in the laboratory. Of course, they cannot create a real tsunami in the lab because of the wave's great size. However, scientists can produce models of tsunamis scaled down to a smaller size, with proportions somewhat similar to those of real tsunamis. This is similar to how aerospace engineers use small-scale models to test airplanes in a wind tunnel. Laboratory testing also helps develop instruments that can better detect tsunamis in the open ocean before they strike land.

DETECTION AND WARNINGS

Scientists typically classify tsunamis as either local or distant: Tsunamis are local when they are triggered close by and distant when they are generated far from the area where they come ashore. A tsunami can be both local and distant, depending on where you are when it hits. For instance, the tsunami that was triggered by the 1964 great earthquake in Alaska was a local tsunami in Alaska, but a distant tsunami when it struck Crescent City, California. Local tsunamis in Japan can trigger distant tsunamis that hit Hawaii and vice versa.

To alert communities about an approaching tsunami, it must first be detected, and then a warning must be sent out. Unfortunately, with a local tsunami, there is often little time for detection or warning. Local tsunamis may strike within minutes after an earthquake or landslide. A distant tsunami may allow enough time for detection and for authorities to send out a warning before it strikes the shore. In 2004, it is estimated that there were two hours between the time the tsunami was triggered off of Sumatra and when it struck Sri Lanka. Unfortunately, at the time, there was no way to warn the people of Sri Lanka or many other communities along the shores of the Indian Ocean before the tsunami struck.

The Indian Ocean tsunami spurred scientists across the globe to work harder to create better and more widespread tsunami warning systems. These systems are designed to detect a potential tsunami and alert coastal communities that one may be on its way. Seismic stations throughout the world constantly monitor for earthquakes under the seabed and transmit data to regional tsunami warning centers, such as the Pacific Tsunami Warning Center in Hawaii or the Alaskan Tsunami Warning Center in Alaska. When an earthquake occurs, the likelihood of its triggering a tsunami is assessed based on its location, depth, and magnitude. In some cases, scientists also take into consideration the history of tsunami generation in the area. If a tsunami is deemed likely, a warning is quickly issued for coastal areas that could be affected within several hours or less. A tsunami *watch* is issued for regions that may be impacted later. Any coastal earthquake with a magnitude of 7.0 or more triggers an immediate tsunami *warning*. Throughout the world, tsunami warnings are now better coordinated between regional centers, and new global cooperation is under way to provide improved warnings internationally, especially in areas that do not have a warning center. Tide gauges measure water levels along the coast. Scientists at the warning centers monitor tide gauges once a warning has been issued to detect changes that might be associated with an approaching tsunami or to confirm that one has or has not occurred.

In the open ocean, tsunamis are more difficult to detect or confirm. Scientists at the National Oceanic and Atmospheric Administration (NOAA) and throughout the world are working hard to develop instruments that can detect tsunamis in the open ocean. NOAA scientists have created a bottom pressure sensor that is designed to measure the pressure changes and wave characteristics associated with the passage of a tsunami at sea. This sensor is part of an instrument package that sits on the seafloor and is connected by a cable to a buoy at the surface. If the sensor detects a potential tsunami, it sends a signal up the cable to the surface buoy. The surface buoy then transmits a signal to a satellite, which transfers the data to a shore-based warning center. These sensors are being deployed mainly in the Pacific and Indian Oceans, with a few in the Atlantic as well.

Scientists also combine data from undersea seismic stations and bottom pressure sensors with computer models to better predict where, when, and how a tsunami may strike. These models can help to identify the areas most at risk, generate appropriate warnings, and assist in making decisions about evacuations.

For tsunami warnings to be effective, local communities must also have the means to receive the alerts and pass them on to the people in the areas at risk, who then need to know what to do. In the 2004 Indian Ocean tsunami, the inability to alert people about the tsunami and the warning signs ahead of time contributed to the tragedy.

In the United States, some communities are becoming tsunami-ready. Geologic evidence suggests that about 300 to 400 years ago, a massive earthquake and tsunami struck the coast of the Pacific Northwest, including Oregon, California, and Washington State. Given its tectonic setting, an offshore subduction zone similar to that which lies off of Sumatra, the region will undoubtedly be hit again. School children and the public in the Pacific Northwest are being taught about tsunamis and instructed where to go should an alert be issued. Mapping of potential flood areas is helping to identify evacuation routes and safe places to go in the event of an approaching tsunami.

Tsunami Warning Signs

"Tilly Smith, a 10-year-old girl from Oxshott, Surrey, England, saved a hundred fellow tourists from the December 26, 2004, tsunami. She urged her family to get off Maikhao beach in Phuket, Thailand, after seeing the tide rush out. Her mother and father alerted others to clear the beach. She learned about tsunamis from an earthquake project that her geography teacher, Andrew Kearney, had her complete at Danes Preparatory School."

—Peter Pissierssens, *London Times*, January 1, 2005

As in the case of Tilly Smith, understanding the warning signs of a tsunami can save your life and the lives of others. If you are at the coast and notice any of the following, you should seek safety inland and go as high up as quickly and as calmly as possible:

- A rapid retreat of the sea. It looks as if an extremely fast, low tide is occurring. Do not go seaward or to the shore to investigate.
- The ground shaking. If you are at the shore and feel the ground shake, it may be from an earthquake that began offshore.
- A loud bang or rushing freight train sound coming from offshore. Scientists are not sure why these sounds sometimes occur, but they have repeatedly been reported just before a tsunami hits.
- A community siren or alert indicating a tsunami warning has been issued.

These warning signs may happen minutes or hours before a tsunami strikes. And tsunamis can often be more than just one wave, so if one does hit, continue to stay in or seek shelter until you are notified that it is safe by emergency personnel.

Education is just as critical as a physical warning system. If you are at the coast and notice any of the warning signs of a tsunami, you should calmly and quickly move inland and to higher ground.

The question is not if another tsunami will strike, but when and where. Tsunamis, like earthquakes, are more likely to occur in certain places, such as in the Pacific, around the Ring of Fire. Tsunamis have also occurred in the Caribbean, triggered by earthquakes in the subduction zone that underlies the Puerto Rico Trench. There has been a huge increase in population and tourism in the Caribbean since the last tsunami struck. If one were to strike now, the devastation would be much worse. Tsunamis have been happening on planet Earth for a very long time and they will happen again.

Volcanoes
Across the Globe

▲▲▲

THERE ARE MORE THAN 1,500 VOLCANOES ON LAND ACROSS THE world. Each year only about 50 of these are active, while most lie dormant, asleep for now. Many of the Earth's volcanoes lie undersea. While some volcanic eruptions are dangerous and violent events that threaten nearby communities, others pose less peril and provide spectacular displays that remind us of the Earth's restless nature.

Today, more and more people around the world live within the shadow of a volcano, drawn by their steep, scenic slopes and fertile soils. The result is that millions of people are living at risk. For some, the dangers are not so great because the nearby volcanoes are well monitored and preparations are in place in case of an eruption. For many others, however, the volcanoes in whose shadows they live go unwatched and so the inhabitants go unprepared. Today, we know a lot more about volcanoes than in the past, and we have better technology to watch and to study them. Much of our improved knowledge has come with our growing understanding of plate tectonics, which controls or influences where most, if not all, volcanoes occur.

A Few Famous Eruptions

A.D. *79, Vesuvius, Italy.* Eyewitness accounts of this volcanic eruption tell of an enormous and violent blast that destroyed the surrounding land and killed thousands of people. The eruption of Vesuvius in 79 A.D. began with a blast of gas and ash that produced a huge, pine-tree-shaped cloud rising skyward. For 11 long hours, ash and rocky debris were ejected high into the atmosphere. In the nearby town of Pompeii, day turned to night as the sky darkened, and ash and rocks rained down. The following night, the towering cloud over the volcano suddenly

(continued)

Hundreds of years after the eruption of Mt. Vesuvius in 79 A.D., archeologists discovered gaps in the ash that proved to be impressions of decomposed bodies. The plaster and resin castings of these impressions provide an eerily accurate picture of the last moments of hundreds of Pompeii citizens.

(continued)

collapsed, and deadly flows of burning gas and ash surged off the volcano's summit. The town of Herculaneum and, later, Pompeii were destroyed by the searing flows. Residents were instantly incinerated or buried under about 10 feet (3 m) of burning volcanic debris. Vesuvius is located behind a subduction zone.

1815, Tambora, Indonesia. This was the world's largest ash eruption ever recorded. During the eruption, huge amounts of material were ejected into and transported throughout the atmosphere. So much ash was in the air that the year following the eruption was called the "Year Without a Summer" because of how it blocked out sunlight and reduced global temperatures. Superheated flows of gas and burning debris also plunged off the volcano during the eruption, and thousands of people were killed. The volcano lies about 180 miles (300 km) behind the Sunda Trench and its underlying subduction zone.

1980, Mount St. Helens, United States. After 123 years of sleep, Mount St. Helens awoke with a vengeance in 1980. It began with swarms of earthquakes indicating that **magma** was stirring below the surface. The earthquake activity increased, small avalanches of snow and ice cas-

MID-OCEAN RIDGES

Deep beneath the sea at mid-ocean ridges, where the Earth's tectonic plates are spreading apart, there are undersea volcanoes. Human eyes, however, rarely see them erupt. Even scientists who use submersibles and remotely operated vehicles to study mid-ocean ridges hardly ever see or record actual volcanic eruptions. More often, they find evidence of a recent eruption, such as very fresh,

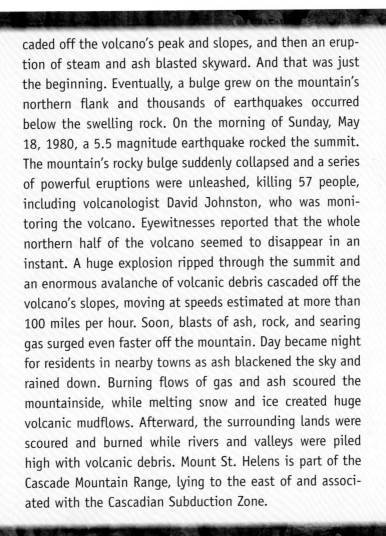

caded off the volcano's peak and slopes, and then an eruption of steam and ash blasted skyward. And that was just the beginning. Eventually, a bulge grew on the mountain's northern flank and thousands of earthquakes occurred below the swelling rock. On the morning of Sunday, May 18, 1980, a 5.5 magnitude earthquake rocked the summit. The mountain's rocky bulge suddenly collapsed and a series of powerful eruptions were unleashed, killing 57 people, including volcanologist David Johnston, who was monitoring the volcano. Eyewitnesses reported that the whole northern half of the volcano seemed to disappear in an instant. A huge explosion ripped through the summit and an enormous avalanche of volcanic debris cascaded off the volcano's slopes, moving at speeds estimated at more than 100 miles per hour. Soon, blasts of ash, rock, and searing gas surged even faster off the mountain. Day became night for residents in nearby towns as ash blackened the sky and rained down. Burning flows of gas and ash scoured the mountainside, while melting snow and ice created huge volcanic mudflows. Afterward, the surrounding lands were scoured and burned while rivers and valleys were piled high with volcanic debris. Mount St. Helens is part of the Cascade Mountain Range, lying to the east of and associated with the Cascadian Subduction Zone.

warm fields of cooling volcanic rock on the seafloor. Upon their return to a research site on a mid-ocean ridge, one scientific expedition found their instruments encased in freshly erupted rock.

Hot molten rock beneath the Earth's surface is called magma. If it erupts underwater or on land, it is called **lava**. Magma is generally a mixture of melted or crystallized minerals and dissolved gases. In the deep sea, the ocean is cold and the pressure

Pillow basalt forms deep under the ocean where the extremely cold temperatures cause the lava to cool very quickly.

is extremely high due to the weight of the overlying water. When fiery hot lava erupts in the deep sea, it immediately comes into contact with this cold seawater at high pressure. This keeps volcanic eruptions in the deep ocean from being explosive. Lava cools so fast in the deep sea that there is no time for crystals to grow. The rocks that form are smooth, rounded, and glassy. These are called pillow lavas or pillow basalts. **Basalt** is a rock that contains up to 50% silica and oxygen along with iron, calcium, and magnesium. The relatively high iron content gives it a dark-gray to black color. A pillow basalt looks something like a huge wad of black toothpaste that has been squeezed from a tube and then hardened and cracked.

At a mid-ocean ridge, there are many cracks in the rocks and underlying seafloor. Seawater can flow down through these cracks and come into contact with hot magma below. When this happens, it can create superheated plumes of mineral-rich fluid that burst like undersea geysers through fractures and chimneys in the seafloor.

Scientists have discovered that many small, shallow earthquakes occur along the mid-ocean ridges. These earthquakes may indicate where and when volcanic eruptions are occurring. At any one time, there may be one or more volcanic eruptions happening somewhere along the 37,000-mile-long (60,000 km) mid-ocean ridge system.

So much basalt is produced by volcanic eruptions along the spreading tectonic plates at the mid-ocean ridges that it is one of the most common rocks on Earth. Scientists also believe that because basalt is similar in composition to what makes up the Earth's mantle, studying these rocks can help us to understand the composition of the planet's interior.

CONVERGING PLATE VOLCANOES

Volcanoes are also found where two tectonic plates converge. Behind a subduction zone, where one plate is being driven down beneath another, there is often a linear chain or arc of volcanoes. Volcanoes associated with a subduction zone make up the islands of the Lesser Antilles in the Caribbean and span across the west coast of Central America. The volcanoes along the edges of the Pacific Plate in the infamous Ring of Fire are also associated with a subduction zone and are some of the world's most active and violent mountains of fire.

Volcanoes are created at a subduction zone as the downgoing tectonic plate sinks into the Earth's mantle. As this plate, or slab, descends into the Earth, the temperature and pressure around it increase. When the slab sinks below about 60 to 90 miles (100 to 150 km), some of the minerals within the descending plate release water. Along with the increasing temperature and pressure, scientists believe that this release of water causes some of the rock to become molten and rise upward as a blob, or plume, of magma. As it rises, the molten material may melt more rock along the way. The magma continues to rise until it reaches the surface, where it breaks through to create a volcano. Behind and along a subduction zone, there may be a ribbon of magma forming as a tectonic plate descends into the Earth's mantle. At spots along this underground ribbon of magma, blobs of molten rock form and rise to the surface where they create a chain or arc of volcanoes.

The lava that erupts from a volcano that lies behind a subduction zone varies in chemical composition. Some of it is made of basalt, like the lava seen at the mid-ocean ridges. A large amount of the magma and rock that is created, however, contains more silica than basalt. The various rocks formed from this mixture are called andesite, dacite, and rhyolite, which are all volcanic rocks with different amounts of silica. Due to their differences in chemical composition, these rocks tend to be lighter in color than basalts. The magma at these types of volcanoes also cools

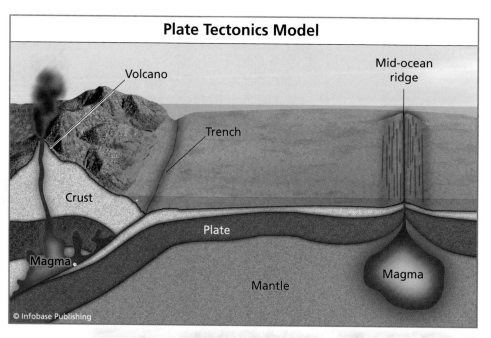

An arc of volcanoes forms behind a subduction zone.

more slowly than at mid-ocean ridges. It may begin to harden, or crystallize, on the way up to the surface. The magma can also melt and mix with the surrounding rock types on the way up. The result is that rocks found at volcanoes behind a subduction zone tend to vary more in composition than those at a mid-ocean ridge.

HOT SPOT VOLCANOES

The third type of plate tectonic setting to produce volcanoes is known as a hot spot. Hot spots occur in the interior of tectonic plates. Scientists do not exactly understand why they occur, but they seem to be located at concentrated areas of heat deep in the Earth's mantle. Hot spots also seem to be relatively stationary,

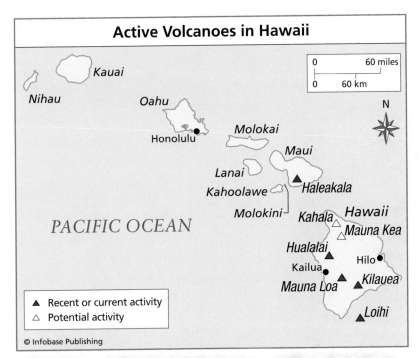

The islands of Hawaii are home to many active and potentially active volcanoes, resulting from the movement of the Pacific Plate over a hotspot.

Mount Kilauea on the island of Hawaii has been erupting regularly for decades. Volcano-watching has become a major tourist attraction for the island.

or unmoving. They are located at specific places where plumes, or blobs of magma, continually rise through the mantle to the Earth's surface to create volcanoes. Because the planet's tectonic plates are continually moving, they are like conveyor belts that pass over these stationary hot spots. As the plate passes over the hot spot, a volcano forms. As the plate continues to move, more volcanoes are created to form a chain of volcanoes.

The Hawaiian Islands are the most well-known example of hot spot volcanoes, formed due to the movement of the Pacific Plate over an underlying hot spot. The Big Island of Hawaii, still moving over the hot spot, has five volcanoes that are considered active or potentially active. Hawaii's Mauna Loa is one of the largest volcanoes in the world at more than 13,000 feet (4,000 m) above sea level. Kilauea is the most active of Hawaii's volcanoes and has been erupting almost constantly since 1983. Kilauea continues to produce massive quantities of red-hot lava that create glowing rivers that stream into the sea and, sometimes, fiery fountains that light up the sky. In addition, a new volcano in the chain is now forming to the southeast of Hawaii. It has been named Loihi and lies more than a thousand feet below the sea surface.

Hot spots can be large and stable for a long period of time, even millions of years. The hot spot underlying Hawaii appears to have been in about the same place for about 70 million years. From Hawaii, a chain of 137 islands and seamounts stretches northwest across the Pacific Plate, all of which were created by the underlying hot spot.

We often think of the hot spot volcanoes on Hawaii as typical volcanoes. This may be because we so often see the fiery show put on by Kilauea in photographs or video. Yet, Hawaii's hot spot volcanoes are anything but ordinary or common. The rocks produced are made of basalt, and the eruptions are never highly explosive. Most volcanoes that erupt on land do not have rocks made of basalt, and eruptions are typically much more explosive.

Some scientists speculate that hot spots were more common in the past. Today, we know of only a few active hot spots, including one beneath the Galapagos Islands in the Pacific and another under the continental crust of the famous Yellowstone National Park in the northwestern United States. There are still many unanswered questions about hot spots: Why are they located where they are? Do they ever move? What causes them to become active?

RIFT VALLEY VOLCANOES

The Great African Rift Valley in East Africa represents another type of plate tectonic setting where volcanoes occur. The history

When tectonic plates move apart, a rift valley forms. The Great African Rift Valley, seen here in Kenya, stretches down the length of East Africa and will someday in the future form the beginnings of a new ocean.

of Africa as a continent is ancient and relatively stable. Now, however, its eastern half is breaking apart. A new area of plate divergence has begun and the African Plate, which includes the entire continent of Africa and surrounding oceanic crust, is literally being ripped in two along the area known as the Great African Rift Valley. The spreading of the plates and the eruption of magma in the Rift Valley has created a series of active volcanoes in the region. Scientists do not know why, or how, new divergent boundaries such as this begin, but we are seeing it happen before our eyes. And millions of years from now, if the rift continues to spread apart, in the middle will be a new ocean with a new mid-ocean ridge.

The volcanoes of the Great African Rift Valley produce magma and rocks that vary greatly in composition. Magma from the Earth's mantle rises into the rift as the African Plate is broken up and the two sides split apart. On its way to the surface, the magma travels through the continent's ancient rocks, melting and mixing with them. This leads to a very complex and variable chemical composition. Some of the volcanoes in the region erupt explosively, while others spew highly fluid lava that can flow unusually fast.

6

Volcano Science

▲ ▲ ▲

SCIENTISTS WHO STUDY VOLCANOES ARE CALLED VOLCANOLOGISTS.
While it is their goal to understand volcanoes in general, these
scientists often focus their efforts on identifying the signs of an
impending eruption and determining how a volcano is likely to
erupt. They also monitor volcanoes across the world for potential
activity and work to assist communities that may be at risk.

UNCORKING A VOLCANO

When a bottle of champagne is uncorked, bubbles rush to the surface and explode out the top. In a simplified way, this is similar to
what happens when some volcanoes erupt. Before it is opened, a
bottle of champagne is full of energy in the form of **dissolved** gas
just waiting to escape. With the bottle tightly sealed by an over-
sized cork, which is wrapped tightly by a wire cage, high pressure
inside keeps the gas dissolved within the liquid champagne. There
are few, if any, bubbles visible. When the cork is popped, the
pressure inside the champagne bottle instantly decreases. Once
that happens, the gas inside comes out of its dissolved state and
forms bubbles. The bubbles form incredibly quickly and rise to the

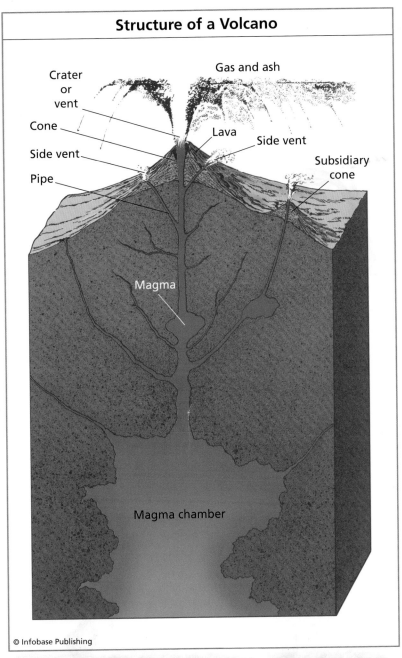

Structure of a Volcano

Crater
or
vent

Gas and ash

Cone

Lava

Side vent

Side vent

Subsidiary
cone

Pipe

Magma

Magma chamber

The internal structure of a volcano shows how magma may move
toward the surface.

surface with enough speed and energy to turn many a champagne cork into a dangerous flying projectile. A volcano can erupt in a similar way, though obviously with much more violence, power, and potential danger.

Volcanoes form where magma lies deep in the Earth under high temperatures and pressures. In addition to melted minerals, magma contains dissolved gases, including water, carbon dioxide, and rotten egg-smelling sulfur dioxide. The gas contained within magma tends to make it less dense than solid rock and more buoyant. This causes the magma to rise up toward the surface through cracks, holes, and fractures in the Earth's mantle and crust. As it pushes to the surface, the molten material may melt or break through rock, or collect in large open spaces or chambers. Gas within the magma may begin to form bubbles (like the dissolved gas in the champagne). These gas bubbles then begin to rise to the surface at a faster rate than the magma. If there is a fracture or crack in the crust, gas, followed by lava, may erupt at the surface. Should there be a tight, rocky seal (or cork) at a volcano's summit blocking the way, however, the gas and magma will begin to collect beneath the surface. A swelling bulge or growing rocky dome on a volcano can be evidence of gas or magma building up below the surface. If too much pressure builds up, or if an earthquake or landslide breaks the overlying rocky seal, an explosive eruption can occur. The size of the eruption depends partly on how much gas, magma, and pressure are released. While a champagne cork can fly violently across a room, during a volcanic eruption, the energy released can cause rocks, hunks of lava, and tons of ash or gas to be ejected high into the atmosphere or to flow swiftly down a volcano's slopes.

TYPES OF VOLCANOES

In some ways, each of the Earth's volcanoes is like an individual person with its own style and personality. No two volcanoes look exactly alike, nor do they erupt in exactly the same way or at the same time. Yet, volcanologists have identified specific character-

Volcanic Explosivity Index

To describe the relative size of a volcanic eruption, some scientists use the Volcanic Explosivity Index (VEI). It ranges from a VEI 0, a nonexplosive, gentle eruption of liquid lava, to a VEI 8, which is a violent massive explosion lasting more than 12 hours. At VEI 5 or higher, an eruption is rated as being very large to cataclysmic. Explosive eruptions of this magnitude have happened, on average, only once every 10 to 20 years. Scientists have studied the historical accounts and geology of about 5,000 eruptions in the past 10,000 years. No eruption within that time period has yet warranted a VEI as high as 8.

As with earthquakes, the magnitude of a volcanic eruption does not necessarily determine its impact or the amount of damage. Volcanic eruptions with a high VEI may do little damage if they take place in an unpopulated region. On the other hand, a volcanic eruption with a low VEI can cause catastrophe if many people are living nearby. For example, in 1985, the eruption of the Nevado del Ruiz volcano in Colombia and the mudflow that followed killed 23,000 people, yet the eruption was rated as VEI 3. The Mount St. Helens eruption was much more violent and ranked as a VEI 5, but because the area was less inhabited, fewer people were killed. The size or explosive nature of an eruption may only be partly a factor in the number of people hurt or killed. The location of the blast in relation to nearby populations is just as important as the type of eruption that occurs. And, of course, how well informed and prepared any local communities are makes a difference as well.

istics that are common among certain types of volcanoes. These common traits are defined by plate tectonics, the style and type of eruptions that occur, as well as the shape of the volcano. This makes sense because volcanoes are landforms built by eruptions; therefore, similar styles and types of eruption produce similar types of volcanoes.

SHIELD VOLCANOES

When most people think of volcanoes, they think of the lava-spewing, blackened domes of Hawaii. Hawaii's mountains of fire are called *shield volcanoes* because their broad, gently sloping shapes look a bit like a warrior's shield. Shield volcanoes form as successive flows of hardened lava build up over time, creating

The massive Mauna Loa shield volcano rises behind the Mauna Kea volcano (*foreground*) in Hawaii Volcanoes National Park, Hawaii.

a wide, domed structure. Lava flows at this type of volcano are typically very fluid, and they spread out over long distances. As these rivers of fiery lava flow down the volcano's sides, they cool and form gently sloping sheets of crusty black basalt. Eruptions at shield volcanoes are rarely explosive. The frequent and easily flowing lava allows gas to escape so it does not build up beneath the volcano.

At the summit of many shield volcanoes is a large circular depression called a **caldera**. Calderas usually form when lava is emptied from an underlying chamber and the overlying rock collapses. Smaller features that are produced by the collapse of rock or explosive eruptions are called craters. Sometimes, lava also erupts from fractures, rifts, or fissures along a volcano's slopes.

In Hawaii, lava and the rocks it creates are generally described as either *aa* (pronounced "ah ah") or *pahoehoe* (pronounced "pah hoi hoi") flows. *Aa* lava is thick, relatively slow moving, and cools to create rough, fragmented, rocky flows. Shoes with tough, thick soles are needed to walk over the sharp, rough terrain of an *aa* flow. *Pahoehoe* flows are thinner, more fluid, and form smooth, ropy rocks. In a cooled *pahoehoe* flow, the streams, swirls, and blobs of the once fluid lava appear to have been frozen in place.

One of the most spectacular sights in Hawaii is when hot lava meets the cold sea. As fiery lava falls into the ocean, it cools extremely quickly and geysers of steam gush skyward. The cooling happens so quickly that the hardening rock may shatter into small pieces of black glass upon contact with the water. As a result, nearby beaches are often lined with shiny black sand. The process is similar to what happens when cold water is poured into a hot coffeepot made of glass. The coffeepot almost always cracks.

STRATO OR COMPOSITE VOLCANOES

Most volcanoes on Earth are not the broad domes of a shield volcano. They typically have steep sides, are more cone-shaped, and have a smaller crater at the summit. These are called *stratovolcanoes*, or composite volcanoes. They are built by successive erup-

There are two main kinds of lava in Hawaii: The chunky, jagged lava in the background is called *aa*, while the thick, ribbon-like lava in the foreground is called *pahoehoe*.

tions that can include both lava flows and more explosive events, which pile up **pyroclastic** debris. Pyroclastic, or pyroclasts, refers to rocky fragments that are blasted out of a volcano in an explosive eruption. They can be as small as tiny ash particles or as large as huge blocks. In especially dangerous and explosive volcanic eruptions, pyroclastic debris can mix with hot gases to create a fast, burning flow that speeds down a volcano's side. These are sometimes referred to as a *nueé ardente*, French for "glowing cloud," or simply a pyroclastic flow. A stratovolcano eruption can be one of the most deadly types of explosions on Earth. Some of the world's most majestic and dangerous mountains are strato-volcanoes, including Mount St. Helens and Mount Rainier in the state of Washington, Oregon's Mount Hood, Japan's Mount Fuji, Italy's Mount Vesuvius, and Indonesia's Krakatau.

Eruptions from stratovolcanoes typically begin with an explosive blast of gas, ash, and rocky debris. Ash clouds may rise high up into the atmosphere. After the gas and gas-rich magma has been ejected, thick, viscous lava may gush out of the volcano's crater. Over time, and with repeated eruptions, layers of debris and cooled lava build up to create a cone-shaped mountain. Magma usually flows through a channel or tunnel beneath the volcano and erupts through a central vent into a crater at the summit or from cracks lining the mountain's sides. The hardened lava that fills these cracks or fissures can help to support and strengthen the volcano's sides. If the volcano's central vent gets plugged, a secondary vent may open and create a smaller volcanic cone nearby.

Volcanoes that lie above subduction zones are of the strato, or composite, type. The lava flowing from their craters or fissures tends to be thicker and less fluid than the flows of a shield volcano, as in Hawaii. In eruptions, light-colored rocks that are riddled with holes and bubbles may be ejected skyward. This type of volcanic rock is called *pumice* and can contain enough trapped gas inside for it to float in water.

An extremely thick lava flow, or an underlying buildup of gas or magma, may create a bulge, or dome, on a composite volcano. Before the powerful eruption of Mount St. Helens in 1980, the bulge on its northern side grew about 450 feet (137 m) high and 85 feet (30 m) wide. The collapse of the lava dome on Mount St. Helens is believed to have been what triggered the devastating blasts and pyroclastic flows that followed.

Volcanoes that have not erupted for a long time are called dormant and may lay quiet for centuries or more. Over time, weathering can erode a dormant volcano's summit, making

In May 1980, Mount St. Helens erupted, covering much of the Pacific Northwestern United States in varying levels of ash.

it look less like a sleeping volcano and more like a harmless mountain. Residents who live nearby may not even realize it is a volcano. This can be especially dangerous should the mountain actually turn out to be a potentially explosive stratovolcano.

Cinder Cones

In the early 1940s, a farmer in Mexico found a mysterious hole in one of his fields and decided to use it as a convenient rubbish dump. In late February 1943, however, his field began to shake and rumble. A large crack appeared across the bottom of the strange hole. Much to the farmer's surprise, the hole then began to belch fire and ash. Within days, a *cinder cone* more than 30 feet (9 m) tall had formed around the hole on his field. It continued to erupt and just one year later his flat, quiet field of corn had become a cinder cone more than 1,100 feet (410 m) high, now named Parícutin.

A cinder cone is built of cinders ejected from a volcanic vent or crack. It is probably the most common and simple type of volcanic structure. The creation of a cinder cone occurs as gas within the erupting magma causes lava to be blown violently into the air, where it breaks up into large particles of ash or cinders. As the cinders cool, they solidify and fall to the ground, thereby accumulating as a circular volcanic cone around the erupting vent. Cinder cones can be created through unexpected eruptions along volcanic cracks, as the farmer in Mexico discovered, though they most commonly occur at fractures or vents on the sides of a volcano. On the flanks of the Hawaiian volcano Mauna Kea, geologists have documented nearly 100 cinder cones.

Flood Basalts

Throughout the Earth's restless history, there have been extensive eruptions of highly fluid, basaltic lava from long fissures in the planet's crust. These create large, flat plains of cooled volcanic rock called flood basalts. Ancient flood basalts form broad, low-lying plateaus in Iceland and near the Columbia River in Washington and Oregon.

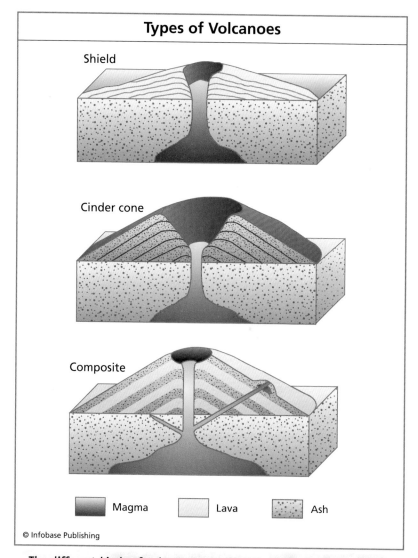

Types of Volcanoes

Shield

Cinder cone

Composite

Magma   Lava   Ash

© Infobase Publishing

The different kinds of volcanoes are classified based on their shape and styles of eruption.

Volcanic Lakes

Some of the world's volcanoes have a lake at their summit, located within the crater, or caldera. Gases, such as carbon dioxide, may enter from the underlying volcano and accumulate within the lake, especially at its bottom. This can create a special, though relatively rare, danger. If a gas-rich volcanic lake is disrupted, it may release its toxic fumes over the nearby lands. This happened in 1986 in Lake Nyos in Cameroon, Africa. The sudden release of toxic gas from the lake caused the deaths of 1,700 people. Volcanic lakes can also be the source of massive mudflows and flooding during eruptions.

READY TO BLOW?

One of the main goals of a volcanologist is to determine if, how, and when a volcano will erupt. The probability of a volcanic eruption is usually calculated based on changes in the volcano's current level of activity. Scientists note these changes by creating, in a sense, a "daily diary" for the volcano. In this "diary," they note repeated measurements of gas emissions at the summit and near fissures. They monitor earthquake activity and the shape of the volcano's summit or slopes. With relatively long-term monitoring, scientists can determine what is the baseline, or "normal," activity for the volcano. Changes from this baseline state might mean that magma or gases are moving beneath the volcano, which could indicate that it is becoming more active. Volcanoes may exhibit signs of unrest months to years before an eruption occurs. This type of monitoring, however, is very expensive and labor intensive and takes equipment and trained, experienced personnel. In many regions of the world, particularly in poorer nations, such volcano monitoring may be impossible or simply be seen as a lower priority when compared to problems such as hunger, water pollution, and disease.

Many volcanologists today focus their efforts on studying and carefully monitoring specific volcanoes to better understand volcanoes in general and to learn what the warning signs of an eruption are in a specific region. Volcano observatories are set up on specific sites to closely monitor and observe volcanoes, especially those that lie near populated regions. While there are many potentially dangerous volcanoes in the world, only a relatively few of them are regularly monitored or studied in depth. Some of the new tools being used to study volcanoes, such as relatively

Cool Tools

Scientists now have a host of high-tech tools to help them poke, prod, and investigate Earth's volcanoes. Modern seismometers used to detect earthquakes are also helpful in the study of volcanoes. Prior to and during an eruption, earthquakes may be triggered as magma or gas moves through the underlying rocks or breaks its way to the surface. Earthquakes can signal that a volcano is reawakening months, weeks, days, or hours in advance of an eruption. Some of these earthquakes happen in swarms of numerous small but unusually long and rhythmic quakes. This is called *volcanic tremor* and is caused by the movement of fluid or gas through cracks beneath the surface. With information from a series of seismometers, volcanologists can also use computers to create a 2- or 3-D image of a volcano's interior.

Volcanologists often outfit a volcano with sensitive instruments to monitor the changing shape of a volcano's summit and slopes. A bulging or growth of a dome on a volcano can be precisely measured with GPS (Global Positioning System) receivers, tiltmeters, and laser technology. (A tiltmeter simply measures the tilt or slope of the ground.) Laser-equipped instruments precisely measure the distance between points on a volcano so that if the distance between two points changes over time, it

inexpensive GPS instruments and satellite imagery, are helping to improve monitoring of more volcanoes, especially those located in areas where access is difficult.

Scientists not only want to predict when a volcano may erupt, but they also want to forecast what type of eruption might occur. Is an eruption likely to entail a slow-moving river of lava or a more deadly and fast pyroclastic flow? If a volcano has erupted in recent history, information on the type of eruption that is likely shows that the land has shifted and that magma may be moving below.

Scientists also use special instruments to measure the concentration of gases emitted by a volcano. Because gas rises through a volcano faster than magma, an increase in gas emissions may reveal significant changes in activity long before an explosive eruption occurs. Instruments to measure gas concentrations can be hand-held, placed on the ground, or can even take measurements from a passing airplane or helicopter. Volcanoes can be a dangerous place to work, and acidic gases can damage sensitive instruments. Scientists must take great caution when collecting samples of gas or rock on a volcano. They often try to deploy equipment or use technology that does not require them to make repeated visits to potentially active sites.

Satellite technology is also providing an exciting and relatively new means to study volcanoes. Instruments onboard satellites can detect high concentrations of sulfur dioxide gas in the atmosphere or changes in the surface temperature associated with volcanic activity. Scientists can also compare detailed satellite-derived images of a volcano to look at precise changes in elevation or the geography of the landscape over time. Satellite technology is especially advantageous for the study of volcanoes located in remote regions and also reduces the amount of time scientists must spend in the vicinity of a potentially dangerous volcano.

to occur may be more readily available. In most cases, however, little is known about a volcano's past eruptions, and scientists must rely on the geology of the surrounding land for information. They may find clues to a volcano's past in buried layers of ash, in pyroclastic debris, or in the remains of a mudflow. By studying the geologic evidence around a volcano, scientists can assess what kind of eruptions have previously occurred, how often they have happened, and what areas may be most at risk in the future.

Volcanic Hazards
and Reducing Risk

▲▲▲

TODAY, SCIENTISTS HAVE BETTER INSTRUMENTS THAN EVER BEFORE TO study and monitor volcanoes. We have a better understanding of how, why, and where volcanoes occur and what the signs of an impending eruption are. We are getting better and better at recognizing the hazards that volcanoes present, and many people are now working to reduce the risks to nearby communities. Volcanic eruptions remain a serious hazard in many parts of the world, however, and many lives could be saved with better prediction capabilities and alert systems. In many cases, scientists and emergency responders have learned from previous disasters in order to respond more effectively and successfully to eruptions that have followed.

Colombia, 1985: Nevado del Ruiz

On the night of November 13, 1985, residents of the small town of Armero, Colombia, had no idea of the tragedy soon to occur, a disaster that may have been preventable.

About 30 miles (48 km) away from Armero sits the crater of the volcano Nevado del Ruiz. In 1984, the volcano began to show signs of activity as it rumbled and spewed ash into the sky. Recognizing the dangers of a potential eruption, Colombian geologists began studying the history of Nevado del Ruiz. They investigated previous eruptions and mapped out the volcanic sediments that had been deposited during previous events. The news was not good. Nevado del Ruiz's previous eruptions had created huge, powerful mudflows that had rushed down the volcano's sides, sped through stream valleys, and buried nearby towns. A map of the dangers posed by this volcano was made to warn and help prepare local townspeople. Sadly, the local authorities paid little attention to the volcanic hazards outlined in the map. All too soon, the predicted dangers came true.

The disastrous eruption of Nevado del Ruiz began with a sudden and powerful explosion that triggered pyroclastic flows of hot gas and debris. These flows melted the extensive fields of snow and ice at the volcano's peak and caused torrents of hot water, sediment, and rocky debris to rush down the volcano's slopes. As water poured down the mountain, more rock, sediment, and trees became mixed in, and an enormous mudflow surged off the volcano. Less than an hour after the initial explosion at the volcano's crater, a deadly river of mud and debris rushed over the town of Armero. More than 20,000 people were instantly buried. Evidence later indicated that in some places, the mudflow was nearly 150 feet (46 m) deep.

An eruption can create a variety of dangers depending on how the volcano erupts and where people are located. Volcanic hazards include powerful explosions, searing pyroclastic flows, massive avalanches, falling ash, and surging mudflows. In rare instances, slower moving lava can also pose a serious threat. The powerful mudflow triggered by the Nevado del Ruiz eruption in 1985 and its tragic consequences were a lesson that scientists and emergency managers took to heart. New strategies were developed to better monitor volcanoes and reduce the danger to those living nearby. In 1991, when Mount Pinatubo in the Philippines erupted, these new plans were put into action.

Philippines, 1991: Mount Pinatubo

Mount Pinatubo lies on the small island of Luzon in the Philippines. For about 500 years, the volcano lay quiet. Many of the nearly 1,000,000 people living nearby in towns, villages, and on a military base may not have even known it was a volcano. With its green slopes and fertile soil, the mountain seemed peaceful and a good place to live. In July 1990, however, all of this began to change when the volcano awakened. Among the events that took place was a major earthquake that rocked the region at a magnitude of 7.8. The volcano then returned to a relatively calm state until March and April of 1991, when rising magma within the volcano triggered numerous small earthquakes and bursts of steam, and produced a crater on Pinatubo's northern flank.

By early June 1991, a dome of swelling magma and oozing lava rose on Pinatubo's summit. On June 12, a spectacular eruption occurred as gas-charged magma blasted out of the volcano, fueling a huge mushroom-shaped cloud of gas and ash that towered into the atmosphere. Three days later, Pinatubo unleashed one of the largest and most explosive eruptions of the century. Ash and gas skyrocketed upward, reaching about 22 miles (35 km) high. The eruption was so big that fine ash was picked up by winds high in the atmosphere and spread across the globe. This is believed to have caused slight cooling of temperatures worldwide. The sky over Pinatubo turned black, and heavy ash and cinders rained down onto nearby villages.

As if the people living there did not have enough problems already, Typhoon Yunya blew into the area at about the same time. Its heavy rains turned the falling ash into something akin to a downpour of wet concrete, while searing pyroclastic flows and huge avalanches of mud and debris flowed off the volcano.

The eruption was cataclysmic, blasting out a huge caldera at Pinatubo's peak and depositing massive amounts of mud and debris in the nearby valleys, streams, and fields. Yet, despite the power of Pinatubo's eruption and the large human population that lived nearby, only 300 people died in what could have been a much greater calamity. Most of those who died were killed when their roofs collapsed under the weight of rain-soaked ash. Pinatubo's eruption was much more explosive and dangerous than the blast at Nevado del Ruiz, but far fewer people were killed. The story of why so few people died in Pinatubo's blast is a testament to the hard work of scientists, the regional and local authorities, and the international community.

In April 1991, when Mount Pinatubo began showing signs of unrest, scientists from the Philippine Institute of Volcanology and Seismology began to monitor the volcano more closely. They established a danger zone around the volcano and brought in experts from the USGS to examine the hazards and likelihood of an eruption. Together, the team of volcanologists went to work, setting up additional monitoring equipment and investigating the geologic evidence from past eruptions. Their data suggested that previous eruptions of Pinatubo had been explosive and had produced huge mudflows. Even worse, measurements of earthquake activity, swelling at the volcano's flanks and summit, and gas emissions all suggested that the volcano was about to blow. Scientists then worked to warn and educate local authorities about the dangers of an impending eruption. Eventually, more than 75,000 people were safely evacuated from the region. Warnings were also sent out to airplanes flying over the area.

The explosive eruption of Mount Pinatubo could easily have caused a catastrophic loss of life. The saving grace came from our improved understanding of volcanoes, our ability to monitor and assess volcanic hazards, and the work that was done to educate, warn, and evacuate those in danger. International cooperation was also a key to saving lives. Today, there are rapid response teams that can provide assistance to regions faced with an awakening volcano. If the early warning signs of a volcanic eruption occur, a scientific team is ready to go, equipped with portable volcano-monitoring equipment and the ability to examine data from satellites orbiting the globe. The scientists work closely with local authorities to assess the danger that is posed and to determine if evacuations are needed.

U.S. Geological Survey Alert System

In the United States, a nationwide alert and notification system has been developed to report the level of activity at a volcano and to provide warnings when needed. The system consists of four alert levels for people on the ground and a color code specifically designed for pilots and the aviation community. Expert scientists determine what the alert levels should be based on their analysis of data from monitoring of a specific volcano or region.

VOLCANO ALERT LEVELS

Normal

Volcano is in typical background, noneruptive state or, after a change from a higher level, volcanic activity has ceased and volcano has returned to noneruptive background state. Aviation color code is green.

Advisory

Volcano is exhibiting signs of elevated unrest above known background level or, after a change from a higher level, volcanic activity has decreased significantly but continues to be closely monitored for possible renewed increase. Aviation color code is yellow.

Watch

Volcano is exhibiting heightened or escalating unrest with increased potential of eruption, time frame uncertain, or eruption is under way but poses limited hazards. Aviation color code is orange.

Warning

Hazardous eruption is imminent, under way, or suspected. Aviation color code is red.

(Courtesy of U.S. Geological Survey)

MAPPING THE DANGERS

A hazard means something that is dangerous. A risk means the possibility of loss or injury. While these two terms seem a lot alike, they are actually quite different. When it comes to volcanoes, the difference is important. That is because although we cannot stop a volcano from erupting (the hazard), we can reduce the risks and loss of life during an eruption.

To reduce the risks during an eruption of a volcano, the first step is to identify what the hazards are and who is in harm's way. To do this, scientists map all of the volcanic hazards within a given region. The map is based on as much data as the scientists can collect about what happened during previous eruptions, the current state of activity, the layout of the volcano itself, and where people live. Should the volcano erupt, the hazards map outlines where and what the dangers could be. For example, during an explosive eruption, large blocks, or "bombs," may be ejected out of the volcano. Typically, large rock falls are a volcanic hazard in areas within about 2 miles (3 km) of a volcano. Small cinders and ash pose a danger within a wider area. Ash falls are especially problematic for communities that live downwind of a volcano or for jets flying in the region.

During the last 15 years, at least 80 commercial airplanes have been damaged by mistakenly flying through a volcanic ash cloud. Large amounts of toxic gases released during an eruption can also be dangerous. In Hawaii, long-lasting eruptions of Kilauea have created a volcanic hazard called volcanically-derived smog, or "vog." This haze of unhealthy air can be created when volcanic gas emissions combine and interact with oxygen, moisture, dust, and sunlight in the atmosphere. Vog has been known to cause breathing problems, kill vegetation, and contaminate drinking water.

A volcanic hazards map is also used to show where lava is most likely to flow. It describes the potential paths of debris avalanches as well as pyroclastic flows. Where ice and snow are found at a volcano's summit or along its slopes, the potential path of dangerous mudflows, also called *lahars*, are an important part of a volcanic hazards map.

REDUCING THE RISK

The best way to reduce risk is to prevent people from living too close to a potentially active volcano and to move people who

U.S. Regions at Risk

Within the United States, there are specific areas in which volcanic activity is most likely to occur. Not surprisingly, the volcanoes in Hawaii are some of the best monitored and studied in the world. Given what we know about these volcanoes, however, unless something unexpected happens, the risk in Hawaii is thought to be relatively low. Nevertheless, taking into account our short history and the comparatively little that we know about volcanoes, some scientists say to expect the unexpected.

More concern exists about the potential for a dangerous eruption in the Long Valley area of eastern California. Just one week after the 1980 Mount St. Helens eruption, this caldera began to show signs of reawakening. The geology of past volcanic eruptions in the region suggests that if Long Valley were to erupt, the blast could be 500 times greater than Mount St. Helens. No definitive evidence of an impending eruption has since been discovered, but earthquakes, land deformation, and gas emissions are being carefully monitored, and an alert system has been put in place.

In the Pacific Northwest lies the Cascade Mountain Range, a chain of mountains that stretches from northern California to British Columbia. There are at least 13 potentially active volcanoes in the Cascade Range, including Mount St. Helens, Mount Rainer, and Mount Hood. These towering and scenic peaks are strato, or composite, are already residing in dangerous areas. Although this sounds simple enough, it may not be possible to move entire communities or convince people that they should not live near a volcano, especially one that has long been dormant. When a volcano does threaten to erupt, however, evacuating those at risk is critical.

The monitoring of volcanoes reduces risk because it can allow an alert to be sent if the warning signs of an eruption are detected.

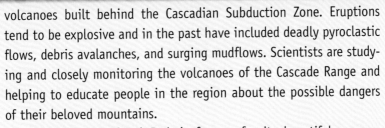

volcanoes built behind the Cascadian Subduction Zone. Eruptions tend to be explosive and in the past have included deadly pyroclastic flows, debris avalanches, and surging mudflows. Scientists are studying and closely monitoring the volcanoes of the Cascade Range and helping to educate people in the region about the possible dangers of their beloved mountains.

Yellowstone National Park is famous for its beautiful scenery, wildlife, and especially its many hot springs, boiling mud pools, and regularly spouting geysers. The park owes its fascinating hydrothermal activity to what lays beneath the ground: a simmering volcano. Scientists now believe that three of the largest volcanic eruptions on Earth took place in Yellowstone. Geologic evidence suggests that during these eruptions, a thick blanket of volcanic ash was spread over much of the western and central United States. The eruptions also produced a huge caldera, tens of miles wide, which formed when an underlying magma chamber collapsed. There has not been an explosive eruption in Yellowstone National Park for thousands of years, and a recent assessment does not predict one anytime soon. Nevertheless, with hot magma still beneath its surface, Yellowstone does pose a volcanic hazard. In 2001, the USGS, Yellowstone National Park, and the University of Utah jointly established the Yellowstone Volcano Observatory (YVO). Scientists are closely monitoring the earthquake and hydrothermal activity, as well as changes in gas emissions and ground deformation in the region. They are also assessing and mapping out the volcanic hazards and have established an alert system.

Today, scientists are working hard to create volcano monitoring systems that link evidence of increased activity or eruptions with specific alerts. At the USGS, a durable and inexpensive instrument has been developed to detect volcanic mudflows. A specially designed monitoring system using these instruments can be put in place on volcanoes where mudflows are likely to happen. Mudflow detection systems have been installed on several volcanoes in the United States, Indonesia, the Philippines, Ecuador, Mexico, and Japan.

Another volcanic hazard monitoring and warning system has been developed to detect ash clouds and alert the commercial aircraft industry. This is necessary because airline pilots on a flight may not be able to tell a volcanic ash cloud from ordinary clouds. Winds can also carry volcanic ash far from an erupting volcano. In 1989, for example, Redoubt Volcano in Alaska erupted. Royal Dutch Airlines Flight 867, a passenger plane on a flight path toward Anchorage, encountered Redoubt's ash cloud. The plane's cockpit filled with foul, sulfur-smelling smoke. Then the engines suddenly quit. The crew struggled to restart the engines and calm the terrified passengers as the plane plummeted about 13,000 feet (4,000 m). Thankfully, they were able to restart the engines and land safely in Anchorage. Damage to the plane was estimated at about $80 million, and all four engines had to be replaced.

Within the North Pacific Region, there are nearly 100 potentially dangerous volcanoes within heavily trafficked flight paths. Scientists and government agencies work together with the aviation community to try to issue timely advisories and alerts about volcanic activity and potentially dangerous ash clouds.

Along with detecting volcanic activity, all warning systems must also include plans for communication. Forecasts of a volcanic eruption and warnings are only effective if they are communicated to the appropriate authorities, who can then make the right decisions to help people and keep them safe. There must be effective communication with the public and local emergency groups. There is also a need for education, so that people understand and take the potential danger seriously and know how to respond should an evacuation be called or an eruption occur.

Volcanologists throughout the world are working to educate local authorities and the public about volcanic hazards, particularly in high-risk areas. This is especially important in regions where nearby volcanoes have been at rest for 100 years or more. People may not be aware of the danger that exists should a nearby mountain come to life. The snow-topped peaks of many majestic mountains may not be as serene and peaceful as they appear.

THE FUTURE

The Earth by its very nature and history is a restless planet. Earthquakes, tsunamis, and volcanic eruptions have been occurring for millions of years. We cannot stop them from happening. We can, however, learn as much as possible about why, where, and how these powerful forces are unleashed. We can identify what the dangers are and who is most at risk. And we can better prepare, warn, and educate people who live in harm's way.

The human population of Earth continues to grow. There are more people living in areas at risk from earthquakes or volcanoes than ever before. That is the bad news. The good news is that through scientific studies and lessons learned from events of the past, we understand more about earthquakes and volcanoes than ever before. A huge step forward came with the revolutionary concept known as plate tectonics. Our technology to study the Earth, earthquakes, and volcanoes has also advanced greatly and continues to progress. In addition to research, scientists now use sophisticated tools to monitor earthquake and volcanic activity. They are also working with local authorities and emergency managers to better prepare and warn people when possible. Throughout the world, people are also being better educated about the dangers of earthquakes and volcanoes, though more needs to be done—much more, as illustrated by the tragic loss of life in China due to the May 2008 7.9 magnitude earthquake and the 2004 Indonesian tsunami.

Unfortunately, we tend to have short memories. Even the most horrific tragedies can be forgotten as time goes by and new people move into areas where a disaster has occurred in the past. We cannot forget the tragedies of the past or simply hope that earthquakes, volcanic eruptions, or tsunamis will not occur. They will, and we need to be prepared. The question is not "Will strong earthquakes happen?" or, "Will volcanoes erupt?" It is: When and where will these events occur on this restless planet we call Earth?

Glossary

▲

Amplitude   A measure of the amount the ground moves as a seismic wave passes by.

Asthenosphere   A layer in the Earth's upper mantle, below the lithosphere, that may be partially molten.

Basalt   A fine-grained, dark rock that has hardened from molten material and that contains up to 50 percent silica and oxygen, along with iron, calcium, and magnesium.

Caldera   A large, circular depression found at the summit of many shield volcanoes, usually formed when the magma from an underlying chamber is depleted, leading to the collapse of the rock above.

Climate   The average and variations in weather that occur over a long period in a region.

Continental   Made of, or related to, the continents, or landmasses, on the Earth's surface.

Continental drift   The theory that the landmasses of the world are capable of moving across the Earth's surface, and that the continents we know today were once part of one supercontinent before breaking apart to drift into their current locations.

Convection   The transfer of heat through movement due to differing temperatures and densities, such as in fluids.

Convergent boundary   Where two tectonic plates are moving toward one another or colliding.

Core   The innermost layer of the Earth. It is most likely made up of a very dense mixture of metals.

Crust   The outermost layer of the Earth and part of the lithosphere. It can be either continental or oceanic.

Crystalline   Made of, or containing, crystals.

Deep-sea trench   A long, narrow, and deep trench in the seafloor, marking an underlying subduction zone.

Dissolved   Absorbed within a liquid solution.

Divergent boundary   Where two tectonic plates are moving away from one another or spreading apart.

Epicenter   The point on the Earth's surface located directly above the underground location, called the hypocenter, where an earthquake starts.

Friction   The resistance, or "stickiness," that is created when one object moves against another object.

Geology   The study of the Earth and its structure, rocks, soils, and minerals.

Groundwater   Water that is underground.

Hydrothermal vent   Fractures in the Earth's surface under the sea; hydrothermal vents emit water that has been heated by molten material or by heat within the Earth.

Hypocenter   The exact location under the Earth's surface where an earthquake originates.

Lava   Magma, or molten rock material, that has erupted on the Earth's surface.

Lithosphere   The outer, rigid shell of the Earth; it is broken up into plates and is made up of the upper mantle and crust; it is located above the asthenosphere.

Magma   Molten rock material within the Earth.

Magnitude   A measure of an earthquake's size.

Mantle   The Earth's rocky interior between the outer core and crust.

Mid-ocean ridge   The undersea mountain chain that forms due to the moving apart of tectonic plates and the creation of new ocean crust.

Mineral A naturally occurring, solid substance found in rocks with a definite chemical composition and an ordered internal structure.

Meteorologist A scientist who studies the Earth's atmosphere, climate, or weather.

Oceanic Of, or related to, the ocean; for example, the oceanic crust is the part of the Earth's crust that makes up the seafloor.

Pyroclastic Made up of fragments or debris from an explosive volcanic eruption, including ash, cinders, or rock.

Sediment Particulate matter that is eroded from rocks and is transported by water, wind, or ice.

Sedimentary Made up of sediments.

Seismic wave A wave of energy that travels through the Earth, typically produced by earthquakes or explosions.

Seismologist A scientist who studies earthquakes or seismic waves.

Seismometer An instrument used to detect, measure, and record seismic waves.

Strain A change in the volume or shape of a rock in response to stress, such as pulling, stretching, or pushing together.

Subduction zone Area where two tectonic plates are converging, with one of them being forced down into the mantle beneath the other.

Submersible A small submarine designed to study or explore the deep sea.

Tectonic plate A section or piece of the Earth's rigid lithosphere that moves relative to the other tectonic plates over the planet's surface.

Transform fault Area where two tectonic plates are sliding past each other in opposite directions.

Tsunami One or a series of waves that are created due to the displacement of water as a result of an earthquake, volcanic eruption, landslide, explosion, or asteroid impact.

Bibliography

▲

Bolt, Bruce. *Earthquakes*. New York: W.H. Freeman, 2003.

Decker, Robert and Barbara Decker. *Volcanoes*. New York: W.H. Freeman, 1998.

Dickinson, William. "A Revolution in Our Time." *Geotimes* 43 (1998): 21–25.

Hough, Susan. *Earthshaking Science: What We Know (and Don't Know) about Earthquakes*. Princeton, N.J.: Princeton University Press, 2004.

Gonzalez, Frank. "Tsunami!" *Scientific American* 280 (1999): 61.

Grotzinger, John, Thomas Jordan, Frank Press, and Raymond Siever. *Understanding Earth*, 5th Edition. New York: W.H. Freeman, 2006.

Kraft, Maurice. *Volcanoes: Fire from the Earth*. New York: Harry N. Abrams, Inc., 1993.

Lay, Thorne, Hiroo Kanamori, Charles J. Ammon, Meredith Nettles, Steven N. Ward, Richard C. Aster, Susan L. Beck et al. "The Great Sumatra-Andaman Earthquake of 26 December 2004." *Science* 308 (2005): 1127-1133.

National Geographic Society. *Restless Earth*. Washington D.C.: National Geographic Society, 1997.

Prager, Ellen. *Furious Earth: The Science and Nature of Earthquakes, Volcanoes, and Tsunamis*. New York: McGraw-Hill, 2000.

Schmincke, Hans-Ulrich. *Volcanism*. Berlin: Springer-Verlag, 2004.

Scientific American Special Edition. *Our Ever Changing Earth.* Vol. 15 (2005).

Sigurdsson, Haraldur. *Encylopedia of Volcanoes.* San Diego: Academic Press, 2000.

Tilling, Robert. "Mount St. Helens 20 Years Later: What We've Learned." *Geotimes* 45 (2000): 15–19.

Tilling, Robert. *Volcanoes.* Denver, Colo.: U.S. Geological Survey, 1997.

Further Reading

▲

Deem, James. *Bodies From the Ash: Life and Death in Ancient Pompeii*. Boston: Houghton Mifflin, 2005.

DK Publishing. *Volcanoes and Earthquakes*. New York: DK Eyewitness Books, 2004.

Kious, W. Jacquelyne and Robert Tilling. *This Dynamic Earth: The Story of Plate Tectonics*. Washington D.C.: U.S. Geological Survey, 1996.

Lauber, Patricia. *Volcano: The Eruption and Healing of Mount St. Helens*. New York: Aladdin Books, 1993.

O'Meara, Donna. *Into the Volcano: A Volcano Researcher at Work*. Kids Can Press, 2007.

Osborne, Mary Pope and Bonnie Christensen. *Pompeii: Lost and Found*. New York: Alfred A. Knopf, 2006.

Patent, Dorothy Hinshaw and William Munoz. *Shaping the Earth*. New York: Clarion Books, 2000.

WEB SITES

There are now many Web sites related to earth science, earthquakes, and volcanoes. Here are just a few that will provide good and reliable information on these important and fascinating topics:

Dive and Discover: Expeditions to the Seafloor
www.divediscover.whoi.edu/
An excellent Web site from the Woods Hole Oceanographic Institution where you can learn about expeditions to the deep sea;

offers especially good information and photographs of hydrothermal vents.

Earthscope Project
www.earthscope.org
The Web site of a national earth science program funded by the National Science Foundation to explore the processes controlling earthquakes and volcanoes.

Federal Emergency Management Agency
www.fema.gov
This site provides excellent information on how to prepare and respond to disasters, such as those that can occur due to earthquakes, volcanic eruptions, or tsunamis.

How Volcanoes Work
www.geology.sdsu.edu/how_volcanoes_work/
An educational Web site, sponsored by NASA, about the science behind volcanoes and volcanic processes.

NASA's Earth Observatory
earthobservatory.nasa.gov/NaturalHazards/
Web site that provides satellite imagery of natural hazards, including volcanoes.

National Oceanic and Atmospheric Administration
www.noaa.gov
NOAA's Web site provides information on research, exploration, and monitoring of our world's oceans, climate, and weather. This site offers good information on tsunamis, waves, hurricanes, and related events around the world.

Seismic Monitor
www.iris.edu/seismon/
An actual monitor, accessible on the Internet, of current earthquake activity worldwide.

USC Tsunami Research Center
www.usc.edu/dept/tsunamis
On this site, one of the world's premier tsunami research groups provides good information on events and ongoing studies.

U.S. Geological Survey
www.usgs.gov

The mission of the USGS includes providing reliable scientific information about the Earth and helping to minimize loss of life and property in natural disasters. Specific information related to earthquakes and volcanoes can be found at www.usgs.gov/hazards, earthquake.usgs.gov, and volcanoes.usgs.gov.

Volcanoes of the World
www.volcano.si.edu/world/

This site provides extensive information about volcanoes across the globe based on data collected by volcanologists working for the Smithsonian Institution. You can search for information on volcanoes in different regions, read about past eruptions, and look at a gallery of photos from volcanoes across the globe.

Volcano World
volcano.und.edu

A collaborative education and outreach project of the North Dakota and Oregon Space Grant Consortia run by the Department of Geosciences at Oregon State University.

Picture Credits

▲

Index

▲

About the Author

▲

DR. ELLEN PRAGER is a marine geologist who specializes in bringing earth and ocean science to the public. She is currently the Chief Scientist for the Aquarius Reef Base program in Key Largo, Florida, which includes the world's only operating undersea research station (www.uncw.edu/aquarius). She has previously worked as a geologist with the U.S. Geological Survey and has published several popular science and children's books about earth and ocean science. She is a frequently requested public speaker and has appeared on national television as an expert when earthquakes, volcanic eruptions, or tsunamis occur.